THE STRANGE DEATH
OF ENGLISH
LEG SPIN

THE STRANGE DEATH
OF ENGLISH
LEG SPIN

HOW CRICKET'S FINEST ART
WAS GIVEN AWAY

JUSTIN PARKINSON

First published by Pitch Publishing, 2015

Pitch Publishing
A2 Yeoman Gate
Yeoman Way
Durrington
BN13 3QZ
www.pitchpublishing.co.uk

A CIP catalogue record is available for this book
from the British Library.

ISBN 978 178531-029-4

Typesetting and origination by Pitch Publishing
Printed in Great Britain by Bell and Bain Ltd, Glasgow

Contents

For Caroline, Iris, Nora

and Grandpa Jack,

and Richie Benaud,

who taught me to love the game

Acknowledgements

FIRST of all I have to thank Roger Packham for poring over my manuscript, searching for errors and suggesting changes. His enormous knowledge of cricket truly is a godsend, as are his enthusiasm and attention to detail.

My good friend Bruce Talbot, an author and chinaman bowler of some repute himself, and cricket literature expert Martin Chandler also gave my words the once-over, which is greatly appreciated. Another good friend, barrister, historian and author Ben Peers, checked out the manuscript.

Paul and Jane Camillin at Pitch Publishing have, as ever, been wonderfully supportive. Thanks also to Duncan Olner and Derek Hammond for their work on the design and presentation of the book, and to Dean Rockett and Graham Hales.

Roger Mann's help with the photographs was invaluable, as were his insights on much of the period covered and on the intricacies of coaching. Nicholas Sharpe gave access to his extensive picture collection, as well as his good advice. My spin bowling protégé (pity him) and photographer James 'Stan' Boardman helped me out as usual.

The writing of *Strange Death* has allowed me to meet several of the best English leg-spinners since the Second World War. Authorship, like leg spin, can be a lonely vocation, so it was a pleasure to discuss cricket with Bob Barber, Robin Hobbs, Warwick Tidy, Andy Clarke, Ian Salisbury, Michael Munday and Matthew Gitsham. They described candidly the difficulties and joys of their art (in their hands it deserves this epithet). They are heroes. England great Ted Dexter kindly took time out to discuss leg spin and his time as chairman of selectors. They were all every bit as entertaining and intelligent as I had expected.

Alastair Peebles and Richard Robins provided insights into their fathers who, I hope, would have found this book worthwhile.

Peter Philpott, probably the world's most esteemed coach and a living god of the pedagogy of leg spin, was a joy to talk to.

Jamie Barker was fascinating on the psychology of leg spin, while Paul Lawrence gave important detail on the life and coaching philosophy of Terry Jenner. Chris Wood of the ECB was informative and friendly, as was Karen Maxwell of the Institute of Groundsmanship.

Bill Parkinson, Nick Clarke, Jon Filby and David Bowden helped put me in touch with Robin Hobbs, Andy Clarke and Ted Dexter. Patrick Ferriday allowed me access to his library. We also had some fun conversations at Small Batch Coffee in Hove.

My visit to the home of David Frith was nothing less than a pilgrimage. He was a kind host and his suggestions were most welcome. Like all good leggies, David not only knows cricket but feels it. How fortunate aspiring cricket writers are to have him to consult.

Neil Robinson and Robert Curphey welcomed me to the MCC library, where I spent many happy hours. The staff at the British Library were helpful, as was Vastiana Belfon at St Mary-at-Hill Church. Once again, Rob Boddie of Sussex County Cricket Club's museum offered access to its archive.

The Guardian's esteemed theatre critic Michael Billington was encouraging and it was good to gauge his views on his boyhood hero, Eric Hollies. I had a splendid few minutes talking to John Mullan, head of English at UCL, about his love of leg spin when we met by chance in the green room at *BBC World* and enjoyed his follow-up e-mail on the subject. It turned out we were both self-taught and of a similar standard!

Steve Hollis of the *Brighton Evening Argus*, a fellow leg-spinner, was a useful sounding board for my ideas and Matt Thacker, by publishing a leg spin-related article in *The Nightwatchman* magazine and asking me to speak about it at the Cheltenham Literary Festival, allowed me to clarify my ideas. Sue Inglish and Alex Hunt, my bosses at the BBC, were also supportive.

Most of all I want to thank my family – Caroline, Iris and Nora – for being so understanding whenever I disappeared to the study for a couple of hours to beaver away on writing some chapter or other. I love you all.

I'll never get to meet the likes of Bernard Bosanquet, SF Barnes, 'Tich' Freeman, Ian Peebles, Walter Robins, 'Father' Marriott, Eric Hollies, Roly Jenkins and so many others, but their writings and the interviews they gave were invaluable sources. They deserve to be remembered.

Introduction

S HANE Warne was almost spent. Australia were about to lose. It was at Trent Bridge in that crazy, dreamlike summer of 2005. Warne was fighting like hell to ensure the Ashes stayed with his team. Through graft, guile and explosive power he managed eight wickets in the match. But for once it was not enough.

As England chased under 130 to win, with the brash South African import Kevin Pietersen steadying the team's nerves, something remarkable happened. England's Barmy Army, who for 12 years had taunted Warne about his weight, his sexual exploits (real and imagined) and his hair (real and restored), thanked him. To the tune of a football terrace song usually directed at unpopular referees, they chanted, 'We wish that you were English. We wish that you were English.'

Warne was visibly moved by their belated generosity of spirit. The crowd applauded a glorious career. But perhaps it was, for once, not all about the man, but the ball. The chants felt like a prayer of thanks for his craft, which he had raised to an art.

Warne had reinvigorated the most beautiful form of bowling. He had as near as dammit perfected leg spin. His place in cricket history was assured, having taken more than 500 wickets with swerve, turn and myriad variations.

England were en route to winning the Ashes for the first time in almost two decades, with a thriller at the Oval still ahead. Yet, as the spectators might have recognised themselves if removed from the euphoria, Michael Vaughan's team were doing it in a very 'English' way.

The batting, admittedly, exhibited more flair and attacking intent than that of most England teams. But the bowling was based on a quartet of fast or medium-fast bowlers: Steve Harmison, Andrew Flintoff, Matthew Hoggard and Simon Jones. Left-arm spinner Ashley Giles kept the runs down in between.

Warne, by contrast, almost held the Australian team's challenge together on his own, taking 40 Test wickets that summer. It was, in personal terms, to be his best series, and, in team terms, his worst.

The Nottingham crowd realised they were watching the passing of something special. We all wished Warne, or someone half as good, could be English.

****

It had all been rather different in another Test seven years earlier. At Headingley in 1998 England's leg-spinner Ian Salisbury was not having so good a time of it. In the previous match at Trent Bridge, South African captain Hansie Cronje had launched a targeted attack on his bowling, pulverising his ego with each blow. He had gone wicketless.

But the selectors, who had picked and dropped Salisbury several times since his debut in 1992, retained his services. Most of the media were unsupportive, disdaining this most likeable of players. Now, as captain Alec Stewart brought him on for a spell, the Leeds crowd joined in the abuse. They booed Salisbury. To the same tune that would later be used to fete Warne, a section also chanted, 'You're worse than David Beckham. You're worse than David Beckham.'

Beckham, the Manchester United and England midfielder, was not popular in the summer of 1998, to put it mildly. He had been sent off in a World Cup football match against Argentina for a petulant foul on an opponent. He had borne most of the blame for the subsequent defeat in a penalty shoot-out. Crowds had gathered at some English grounds to hang and burn effigies of Beckham. His redemption was still far off.

Now Salisbury was being compared to him – and found wanting. A good county bowler, he was the only full-time English exponent of leg spin left in the first-class game. Rather than welcoming a taste of the exotic, the crowd taunted him as an inept bogeyman. It was cruel, a form of cricketing philistinism, even vandalism.

Salisbury's fate was not an isolated attack on leg spin. It was a symptom of almost a century of growing mistrust.

Once, almost every county had at least one leggie, sometimes as many as five. Now they were a highly endangered species in England. They had, Salisbury and a couple of occasionals apart, died out.

****

The inter-war Australian leg-spinner Bill O'Reilly, rated by team-mate Don Bradman as the best bowler in history, spent much of his life bemoaning England's attitude to leg spin. Nearing his final days, he wrote of the country's administrators, 'They could not handle it, so they decided to destroy it.'

He had a point. Almost every major change to English cricket during the 20th century militated further against its success. Rules altered in favour of quick bowlers and off-spinners. Captains became obsessed with containment rather than attack.

By the time Salisbury came along, and even more so as he was progressively overshadowed by Warne, England had developed a national inferiority complex about leg spin.

Surely we couldn't emulate this magician from Australia. It just was not our thing and we should leave it at that. Wait for the batsman's mistake. Play it safe. Look for the percentages.

English cricket had lost any tradition of leg spin, treating it by turns as atavistic, quixotic, expensive, over-flamboyant, impossible to replicate at its best. It faded as we watched, or chose not to see. Whether by cock-up or conspiracy, it happened.

****

Why did English leg spin die?

What happened to the legacy of men like Tommy Mitchell, Ian Peebles, Walter Robins, 'Tich' Freeman and 'Tich' Richmond (leg spin discriminates less than most bowling types on grounds of height), Richard Tyldesley, Len Braund, Doug Wright, 'Father' Marriott, Jim Sims, Bob Barber, Tommy Greenhough, Robin Hobbs, Eric Hollies, Roly Jenkins, Warwick Tidy and Douglas Carr?

What of the heritage bequeathed by the amateur innovator Bernard Bosanquet, who created the craze for googly bowling? And the man I posit as Warne's greatest rival as a bowler of leg breaks, Staffordshire's Sydney Barnes?

In the early 20th century these two English players reinvented leg spin, showing what could be achieved by adapting a style with roots stretching back into the sparsely documented 18th century. Yet the rest of the world, Australia in particular, caught on and overtook the Old Country. In England, leg spin's decline was relative and absolute. We turned away from away turn.

****

Many English leg-spinners have suffered a less brutal form of the ignorance experienced by Salisbury at Headingley on that day in 1998. From club to Test team, they have been misunderstood by captains and spectators, treated like oddities.

I have to confess a personal agenda in tracing the origins and continuation of this attitude. In the summer of 1990, shortly after my GCSE exams, I happened upon a book called *Imran Khan's Cricket Skills*. As I sat on a bench outside Hove Crown Court to read it, I experienced a cricketing epiphany. There, on pages 70 to 73, was something I, a useless batsman and too small to bowl with any pace, might have a chance at. Imran pointed out, step-by-illustrated-step, how his colleague Abdul Qadir was able to torment the world's best batsmen with deliveries called the leg break, googly and top spinner.

Simply by twisting his wrist and fingers, he did all this. The leg break moved away from the right-hander. The top spinner, by a slight turn of the wrist to point the seam down the pitch, dipped more in the air and bounced straight into the batsman's midriff. The googly, by a further turn of the wrist, came in to the right-hander, the ball delivered from the back of the spinner's hand. And it all looked the same to all but the best batsmen.

The varieties came under the heading of 'wrist spin', rather than the more mundane 'finger spin' of ordinary off-spinners and slow left-armers. There was even a ball called the flipper, which involved giving the ball some backspin and skid with a sort of backward, well, flip of the hand. Anyone serious about learning about these deliveries should read Peter Philpott's classic *The Art of Wrist-Spin Bowling* or watch Richie Benaud or Terry Jenner displaying it on *YouTube*.

I persisted with leg spin and, during my late teenage years and early 20s, developed what I now see, from the more distant perspective of having a full-time job and two children, was an obsession. Leg-spin bowling gave me a level of joy I had never experienced. Simply going through the deliveries never bored me. Every summer afternoon became an orgy of net practice.

In some ways the unusualness of leg spin was enjoyable. I liked standing out. But, in other ways, it was agony. I was hit out of the ground, as passers-by laughed at my contortions. In club games, whenever the batsman was on the attack, the exact point when 'buying' a wicket became possible, I was told to keep it tight. With this negative thought in my mind, I bowled worse and worse. And I was taken off.

The problem, I see now, is that I had nothing to fall back on – no leg-spin coaching, no culture of support, no advice. Other than the few hundred words in Imran Khan's book. I did not know then how many others had been through the same experience, including Test match bowlers. I do now.

Imran, who had captained Abdul Qadir through the ordeal of bowling at Viv Richards, included some philosophical advice in his book. Leg-spinners, he wrote, were a 'volatile bunch', adding, 'Perhaps this is understandable, because leg-spin bowling is the hardest type of bowling to control, and when things are going wrong for a leg-spinner they go totally wrong. On the other hand, when things are going right, there is a great deal of satisfaction to be gained from wrist-spinning.'

That is the nub of the style: frustration. It is bloody difficult to get right. The problem is that English cricket, particularly at a high level, is not enamoured of things going totally wrong, or even the risk of things going a bit wrong. We tend to go for conventional seam and off-spin bowlers who keep things tight. These styles, and the discipline involved in them, are admirable. Yet are they not, when taken to extremes, a little monotonous?

Leg spin in this country has long faced a struggle for recognition and understanding, as cricket has undergone its own Reformation. If getting wickets is the God of bowlers, then medium-fast bowling is a form of Puritanism – no frills. Fast bowling and off spin are more on the evangelical side of Anglicanism – a little more levity but still with a directness of purpose. To continue the analogy, leg breaks, googlies, top spinners and flippers, at least when purveyed in the wristiest, most flamboyant style, are the highest of High Church deliveries – all incense, incantations, ceremony and grandeur.

Such festivity is, to my mind, a manifestation of humanity, a reminder that we are more than robots. We need fun and variety to make our often mundane lives palatable. The same applies to cricket.

Father Marriott, who played for Kent in the 1920s and 1930s and took 11 wickets in his only match for England, once wrote, 'The man who has at some time spun a good leg break knows a world all of its own.'

It is a world most of us have lost.

Overarm, Undervalued

*'One might as well whistle
for grouse at the end of November to
come and be shot!'*

Allan Gibson Steel

O NCE, leg spin seemed natural for the English. As bowling moved in the 18th century from being a two-dimensional to a three-dimensional business, it felt right. The ball was no longer to be rolled along as quickly as possible along often bumpy ground, like a rudimentary form of crown green bowls, but tossed up, allowing the vagaries of length, flight and deviation upon landing to come in to play.

The players of the 18th century realised there were possibilities as a result of such innovation. They started twisting the ball, using the seam to achieve a controlled form of sideways movement.

What we now know as leg spin – movement aimed at inducing turn from the leg side to the off to a right-handed batsman – felt more comfortable than the opposite off-spinning effect. The ball sat nicely in the hand and the fingers gave a controllable twist to bamboozle the batsman.

Tom Boxall of Kent is acknowledged by David Frith, cricket's foremost modern historian, as the first 'respectable' proponent of underarm leg spin. The game continued to move on. MCC legalised roundarm bowling in 1835. This was usually delivered from around the wicket to avoid punching the umpire.

In an 1848 handbook he produced, William Lillywhite, one of the best roundarm bowlers, wrote, 'By holding the ball slightly askew, with the thumb well across the seam, you will find by working the wrist as the ball leaves the hand, that it will assist you to cut and rick at the wicket, such balls that are very troublesome to get rid of.'

Bowlers started looking for the elusive 'blind spot', the part of the pitch a few feet in front of leg stump from which the ball turned to hit off stump, or get an edge. David Frith's *The Slow Men* and Amol Rajan's *Twirlymen* give an excellent overview of this developmental period and indeed of the entire history of spin bowling.

W.G. Grace, perhaps the most famous cricketer in history, bowled roundarm leg breaks, often in an effort to buy wickets with men standing on the leg-side boundary. He employed subtlety, with some arguing that he delivered an early form of the flipper, as he sought to deceive batsmen, no doubt overwhelmed by his reputation. C.B. Fry wrote that he got 'drag spin by turning his hand the reverse way and cutting under the ball'.

It was only as arms started to get higher throughout the 19th century, eventuating in MCC agreeing in 1864 that to bowl fully overarm was legal, that leg spin lost its primacy among slower bowlers. Grace, incidentally, did not start his first-class career until 1865, but stuck with the older style.

After the law change, pace bowling, with its ability to control scoring rates, became easier, as did off spin. Off spin seemed to fit in with the mechanics of the more side-on bowling position coming into vogue. It had been difficult, some current theorists argue impossible, to bowl it with any real spin with the arm horizontal. Try it. In contrast, the overarm off-spinner's action allowed rotations in opposition to the movement of the body away from the wicket. Bowled side-on, it was ergonomically efficient and simple to control.

Leg spin, its associations with a bygone age still strong, gained more of an air of imperfectability – of uncertainty – than it'd had during the underarm and roundarm eras, when the accuracy of the best performers was legendary. In 1888, the *Badminton Library of Sports and Pastimes* described overarm leg spin as 'most difficult for a bowler to master'. Some, it acknowledged, had become 'fairly proficient' by this stage, but bowling over after over of leg breaks meant the style lost its 'sting'. In a memorable phrase, this weighty book stated, 'One might as well whistle for grouse at the end of November to come and be shot!'

As early as this point in cricket's development, Englishmen had developed doubts about leg spin. The co-author of the *Badminton* book was Allan Gibson Steel. It is not a name known to many these days, but Steel was a giant (figuratively rather than physically, as he was a small man) of the late 19th century cricket scene. This Lancastrian, a scorer of eight first-class centuries, including two in Tests, was an all-rounder only a peg or so down from W.G. himself. And what was it that made him an all-rounder? Leg spin.

Born in Liverpool in 1858, one of several cricketing brothers, Steel is regarded as the first man to bowl overarm leg spin in international cricket. He was a prodigy at Marlborough College, one of his masters considering him among the best bowlers in the world while still a schoolboy. Steel managed to spin the ball both ways, using conventional leg breaks and off breaks. With a deceptive action, he maintained a good length, putting in the odd faster ball.

In 1878, his first full year playing for Cambridge University and Lancashire, he took 164 wickets at an average of just 9.43. The next three years, for university and county, were almost as successful. In 1880 he made his Test debut at the Oval, getting Australia's Billy Murdoch out for a duck with his fourth ball. It has been described as the first Test wicket for a leg-spinner. But after a few seasons Steel's bowling faded.

In all, he took 789 first-class wickets at 14.78, including 29 in Tests at a shade under 21. He achieved notable deeds, but was preoccupied in his book by the apparent limitations of leg spin. *Wisden* hinted at the reasons why when it said Steel's bowling 'owed its success to a certain trickiness, with the usual result that as batsmen found his tricks out, so did he become rather less effective'.

Steel lost the bowler's greatest weapon: surprise. Batsmen became more used to his style and adapted accordingly. Leg spin, in an era when bowling was moving on quickly, looked like an intellectual dead end. 'It is always a slow ball,' wrote Steel, 'as to bowl it fast with any accuracy of pitch is an impossibility – at any rate, it may be assumed to be so, as no bowler has ever yet appeared who could bowl it otherwise than slow.'

Steel's stated methods relied on a cunning and a lack of precise footwork on the batsman's part. 'The trap laid for the batsman in this style of bowling is the danger he incurs unless he is actually to the pitch of the ball,' he wrote. 'If he falls into the snare, the ball is certain to go up in the air owing to the twist of the ball causing it to hit the side rather than the centre of the bat.'

By 1885 his bowling was a 'spent force', according to the historian H.S. Altham, although he noted, 'Even today he must be written down as the best leg-break bowler in history.' This statement was published in 1926.

The sometimes turgid English pitches of the late Victorian era were seen to nullify leg spin, allowing only slow movement off the pitch. More importantly, Steel regarded leg spin as a style which had reached its peak many years before. In his mind the transformation from underarm to overarm had reduced its attacking potential.

He noted that roundarm players of yesteryear 'used to bowl with a considerable bias from the leg side, and were also of well over medium pace'. But those of his generation could not do so.

The movement of the overarm delivery allowed more turning of the shoulder and wrist than had been possible roundarm. This was the birth, in essence, of what we call 'wrist spin' (sometimes misleadingly – not all bowlers attempting such movement use their wrists very much, as we shall see), the generic term for leg spin and the left-armer's version, the chinaman, which comes back in to the right-handed batsman. More action on the ball was possible, but accuracy would be more difficult as the movement was less straight, less linear. The extra sideways work demanded of the wrist also slowed things down.

In Steel's mind overarm leg spin was doomed to be slow and speculative. And Steel's mind itself had neither of those unwanted qualities. Working in his native Lancashire, he became an eminent barrister and, afterwards, the Recorder of Oldham. There is a sense that, after his burst of youthful brilliance, Steel became intellectually unstimulated by his cricketing craft and felt he had better things to do with his time than develop it further and keep his combative edge. He was a brilliant man but his vision was limited, in that lawyerly way, to a development of precedent.

Towards the end of the 1895 season another amateur, 18-year-old Charlie Townsend of Gloucestershire, burst into life. Getting huge turn, he took 131 wickets at just 13.94. He had five good years and continued steadily until 1905, although only playing sporadically for the last few years. He made a brief comeback in 1921 and ended up with 725 first-class wickets, including three in Tests. Townsend was also a good batsman and, like Steel, a lawyer. He became the official receiver at Stockton-on-Tees.

Steel was not alone among the cricketing intelligentsia of his day in doubting the possibilities of leg spin. Kumar Shri Ranjitsinhji talked in detail about the state of the game in his *Jubilee Book of Cricket*, published in 1897, nine years after Steel's book. Helped considerably in its writing by Sussex and England team-mate C.B. Fry, he described successful bowlers of Steel's style as rare. 'Very few bowlers can command both breaks. Those who can are very useful to a side.'

The mistrust shown by Steel continued in Ranji's words. 'Leg break is artificial rather than natural, and is much more difficult to produce than off break. Hence it is not surprising that exponents of it are rare, at least successful exponents… Even the best leg-break bowlers are in the habit of sending down a considerable number of loose balls. However well they bowl, they are liable at times to unmerciful punishment. Sometimes they are extraordinarily successful.'

It was tantalising, but a harder, more professionalised attitude to bowling was taking hold. 'Good wickets...are now almost universal; so mere pace and attempts at break are rendered more or less harmless,' wrote Ranji/Fry.

This is somewhat ironic as one of Ranji and Fry's Sussex colleagues was at this stage beginning to hustle overarm leg spin along a little. Joe Vine – also an attacking professional batsman who was ordered by opening partner Fry, the amateur, to hold an end up while he played the shots – was more rapid than previous leg-spinners. Vine managed 685 wickets in his career, a more than decent sideline.

Named one of *Wisden*'s Cricketers of the Year in 1906, Vine did not play his two Tests until six years later. 'He is essentially a county cricketer,' *Wisden* noted, 'nearly all his work having been done for Sussex, but if, in addition to his batting and fielding, he had managed to retain his skill as a leg-break bowler it is quite likely that he would before this have played for England. Unhappily... Vine soon lost his peculiar gift, knack, or whatever it may be called.' The reason for his decline as a bowler is a mystery, but it seems Vine used leg spin early in his career as a form of expression to compensate for Fry's restriction on his batting. There is a hint of a thwarted maestro straining to do something above the workaday. He never bowled in Tests.

Another all-rounder, Len Braund of Surrey and Somerset, was not a man to be restricted by anyone. This cheerful extrovert was slower through the air than Vine. He bowled very accurately and became a regular England player, featuring in 23 Tests.

'Braund was the greatest gentleman in cricket, either amateur or professional, I ever met,' wrote Cecil Bennett, captain of the Cambridge University side he coached in 1925. Fry described him as 'a most valuable member of the England team and as cool as a cucumber'.

Braund was involved in perhaps the most dramatic moment in England's cricketing history in 1902. In a tight contest, Australia were in danger of total collapse when skipper Joe Darling scooped one of Braund's leg breaks into the air, only for the catch to be dropped by debutant Fred Tate, stationed by the boundary. This let-off proved to be the difference that allowed the Australians to take the series. In one of *the* moments in Test match history, English leg spin succeeded, only for the plan to be foiled by Tate, a butter-fingered off-spinner.

Another player of a slightly earlier time causes some confusion. Surrey and England's George Lohmann was, in statistical terms, the best Test bowler in history. Making his debut in 1886, with Steel as captain, he ended up with 112 wickets at the stupendous average of 10.75. Lohmann bowled at a varying pace, from slow to lively medium. But did he bowl a leg break?

By the mid-20th century, Australia's Bill O'Reilly described Lohmann as one of the pioneers of leg spin at Test level and some subsequent writers have agreed. But Steel wrote in the *Badminton* book that leg spin had to be slow, a few years after Lohmann had first appeared on the scene. It does not seem that he saw him as a fellow leg-spinner. Nor did another of Lohmann's contemporaries, C.B. Fry. 'George did not bowl leg breaks,' he wrote in 1956. 'He relied on his flight, accuracy and subtle variation of pace; and he bowled at the off stump and just outside it.' So what was Lohmann doing?

It seems he was mixing up slower off breaks with quicker balls, either straight or off-cutters. There is a suggestion he moved the odd one away from the batsman with a leg-break action, but that this was rare. Fry's analysis comes across as more or less correct. Lohmann does not belong in the leg spin category.

The varieties used by most genuine leg-spinners, like Steel, were the off break and quicker ball. There are suggestions of some bowlers trying other variations, by occasionally turning the wrist over more to get the ball to spin in towards the right-handed batsman, or giving it an underhand flick to help it skid on, like Grace. But, on the whole, experts thought Steel's words were true and that leg spin involved no more inherent variety than any other type of bowling – except those of line and length. It had not kept pace with cricket's 'march of intellect', the satirical phrase first used to describe the movement to the roundarm style in the early 19th century. In fact, leg spin had lost pace and controllability in the transition from roundarm to overarm.

During the early 20th century assumptions of limitation were to be challenged, with two very different Englishmen leading the charge. One was Bernard Bosanquet, usually referred to as the inventor of the googly but better described as its revealer, developer, explainer or populariser. The other was a man more often regarded as the best medium-pacer in history, Sydney Barnes.

Between them they added new dimensions and speeds to leg spin. In doing so they thrilled the cricketing world. But others got better at it, while the English stagnated and regressed. By the time Steel died in June 1914 the beginnings of this negative development were under way.

The historian George Dangerfield, in his book *The Strange Death of Liberal England*, wrote about the Liberal Party's demise after its greatest success – getting the Parliament Act passed in 1911, giving the House of Commons lasting primacy over the House of Lords.

'From that victory they never recovered,' Dangerfield remarked. After Bosanquet and Barnes, neither did English leg spin.

A Gift Squandered

'I am responsible for you.'

Bernard Bosanquet to
Clarrie Grimmett

L EG spin was, by the end of the 19th century, no longer the 'natural' method of applying sideways movement to the slowly delivered ball. Off spin had taken on this label, as had its mirror style – orthodox slow left-arm spin. Even Allan Gibson Steel had dismissed overarm leg spin as a limited weapon against the best batsmen once novelty was lost.

Yet, as the long reign of Queen Victoria moved into that of her bacchanalian son Edward VII, these two qualities – novelty and unnaturalness – came together in a way quickly deemed revolutionary, dastardly, untrustworthy and ungentlemanly. Like the crowd at an East End freak show watching the veil removed from a bearded lady, the cricketing world stood reviled but enticed as the actions of its apparent progenitor proclaimed, 'Behold the googly.' To this day to 'bowl someone a googly' means to deceive. In Steel's time, leg breaks, interspersed with off breaks, were only seen as deceptive in that speeds, amounts of flight and degrees of turn could be varied. His intellectual universe did not extend beyond this and he tired of the bowling style he had done so much to pioneer.

Some bowlers had been able to turn the ball in towards the right-handed batsman with an apparent leg-break action. Among them was Jim Phillips of Middlesex, although *The Times* said his length was 'poor, and, as he received little encouragement from those in authority, he gave up practising'. Walter Mead, who played for Essex from 1892 to 1913, did the same occasionally. But, like Steel, he usually preferred off breaks, deemed 'splendid' by *Wisden*, for variation.

It took someone with confidence and a fertile imagination to develop the sort of delivery Phillips and Mead had skirted with and take it further. That someone was Bernard James Tindal Bosanquet. A man of Huguenot descent, he was an archetypal turn-of-the-century cricketing dilettante. An Eton education provided him with a solid training in games. One of the attractions of the school was a billiards table. This luxurious facility allowed the playing of a game named 'twisti-twosti'. Sometimes also known as 'twisty-grab', 'tisty-tosty' or 'fizzle-fuzz', it involved throwing the ball underarm to the other end of the table and putting a break on it so as to deceive the opponent and get it past them. Players had to remain seated throughout. Contests were one-against-one or in teams of two.

'As with bowling at cricket, service, and many other things, length is the first and foremost requirement, and length combined with spin and twist the most deadly,' wrote an anonymous correspondent to *The Times* in 1919. 'I will defy nine people out of ten to tell which way it is going to break,' they added.

In the pantheon of youthful rebellion twisti-twosti ranks somewhat below the defiant magnificence of Marlon Brando in the 1953 biker film *The Wild One*. When asked what he is rebelling against, his character, Johnny Strabler, happily terrorising cafes with his outlaw buddies, replies, 'Whatta ya got?' But in 1911 twisti-twosti provoked its own minor moral panic, at least within one *Times* reader. He complained that the craze for the card game bridge was breeding indolence among the young. They were deserting the game of billiards. The tables of England's great houses vacant, a 'graceless generation' was taking over the baize with 'alien games' like twisti-twosti, showing a disdain for established, codified rules. Bosanquet, like other upper-class youths of the period, became adept at the wiles of twisti-twosti. Perhaps it gave him a sense that the old order could be challenged. Like Brando, his enemy was the status quo.

Even within the deviant world of twisti-twosti Bosanquet rebelled. He noticed that he could turn the ball like an off break by using the leg break action, simply by twisting his hand around in the act of delivery, so that the back of the hand faced his opponent. He wondered whether this idea might have some use in his favourite outdoor ball sport: cricket.

'At first I could only do it underhand,' Bosanquet wrote in an article in 1906, 'but after a great deal more practice was able to achieve it overhand at "stump cricket", first with a tennis ball, and afterward with a ball made of nearly solid India rubber.'

By the time he got to Oxford University, where more thought-permitting leisure time beckoned, Bosanquet was a medium-fast bowler and an unorthodox but effective right-handed batsman. He made his debut for the Dark Blues in 1898. The mystifying principle of his twisti-twosti breakthrough stayed with him.

By 1899 he had 'become a star turn for the luncheon interval'. Bosanquet invited the best batsmen among Oxford's opponents to the nets and bowled them a few leg breaks. 'These were followed by an off break with more or less the same action,' he wrote. 'If this pitched on the right place it probably hit him on the knee, everyone shrieked with laughter, and I was led away and locked up for the day.'

This as yet unnamed delivery involved holding the ball in roughly the same way as a leg break but, at the point of release, turning the wrist right around so that the back of the hand, rather than the front, faced the batsman. The effect was to apply off spin which looked to the unsuspecting like a leg break. It was all a bit of a laugh, but Bosanquet continued to practise it in the nets at The Parks and Lord's, home of his county side Middlesex. It beat bowling quicker 'under a sweltering sun, on a plumb wicket', he reasoned.

Bosanquet began to experiment with this new ball in minor matches and then to use it in first-class games. His first recorded dismissal of a top-class player with what became known as the googly happened at Lord's in July 1900, his victim Leicestershire's Sam Coe. The ball reportedly bounced four times, still a legal delivery in those days, before the startled batsman was stumped for 98. 'The incident was rightly treated as a joke, and was the subject of ribald comment,' noted Bosanquet, 'but this small beginning marked the start of what came to be termed a revolution in bowling.'

One person who saw beyond the silliness was Bosanquet's Middlesex team-mate Pelham 'Plum' Warner. He encouraged his friend to persist with the delivery and, despite his own burgeoning career as a cricket journalist, agreed to keep quiet about it for a while.

'At that time I myself always endeavoured to convey the impression that the result was unintentional and accidental,' said Bosanquet, 'as I did not wish batsmen to be too much on their guard.'

Bosanquet tried his new delivery more often and found that batsmen 'who used to grin at the sight of me and grasp their bat firmly by the long handle, began to show a marked preference for the other end'. Warner recalled that, at first, Bosanquet had been 'laughed at by scores of sound judges'. However, those playing for Middlesex had seen 'enormous possibilities'.

A newspaper cutting from the autumn of 1902 provides a glimpse of Bosanquet's playful mentality. The London-based commercial traveller John George Grant had invented a game called Vigoro, a strange, fast-moving cross between tennis and cricket. Like cricket, it involved bowling, batting and fielding – but all using racquets. The rubber ball was effectively served at the batsman, who hit it with tennis-style shots. Fielding involved bringing the ball to a stop on the racquet and whacking it back in to the middle. Six, instead of the usual three, stumps were placed at each end of the pitch.

Surprisingly, given the potential threat to themselves from an effective merger, the cricket and tennis establishments took to Vigoro, with matches held at Lord's and London's Queen's

Club. Bosanquet played in one between Middlesex and Surrey at London's Crystal Palace just after the end of the 1902 cricket season. New Zealand's *Oamaru Mail*, which had a correspondent present, noted, 'There is just as much variety in the strokes as at cricket, with the additional stroke, played by Mr B.J.T. Bosanquet, the Middlesex cricketer, in the Middlesex and Surrey match, when he hit a fast ball past third man with a back-handed stroke.' Bosanquet was simply, albeit conspicuously, using the variety at his disposal. He learned from tennis, as from twisti-twosti.

Bosanquet was chosen to tour New Zealand and Australia in 1902/03 with Lord Hawke's XI, captained by Warner in the Yorkshire peer's absence. He tried the googly in New Zealand. In one match, Charles Bannerman, the famous Australian who had played in the first ever Test between England and Australia, was umpire. 'When the next team goes to Australia,' he reportedly told Warner, 'be sure that Mr Bosanquet is in it. He bowls a lot of bad 'uns; but that ball of his that breaks the wrong way will be very useful on the hard Australian wickets.'

Warner held Bosanquet back in the first match of the Australian leg of Hawke's tour, against Victoria, allowing him only a few overs. In his description of the match, he indicated why. 'Bosanquet's slow googlies, as they were called in New Zealand, made me blush,' wrote Warner, 'for over and over again the ball pitched three or four times before reaching the batsman, and once he bowled one so wide that [Harry] Graham ran almost to deep point in order to reach it.'

Warner did not use him in the first innings in the next match, against New South Wales. But in the second he let Bosanquet loose. The result was 6-153 off 30.1 overs. He was not accurate, but he could get wickets. The first man Bosanquet dismissed was the brilliant Victor Trumper, bowled by what Bosanquet claimed, in contradiction of Warner's report on the Victoria match, was the first googly ever seen in Australia.

The Duff brothers, Reggie and Walter, were now at the wicket 'and the rate of scoring fell off a lot', the *Sydney Morning*

Herald said. 'The newcomer [Walter] did not display too much confidence in facing Bosanquet.' It is hardly surprising. Warner had left some food for nervous gossip among Australians by giving them only a limited view of a bowler who could do such damage on the country's rock-hard pitches. Might he be the man to help regain the Ashes in the next series in Australia?

Against New South Wales Bosanquet bowled well, 'in marked contrast to the awful stuff he had sent down at Melbourne', according to Warner. In mitigation of his inconsistency, it was not just the googly Bosanquet was learning. He was having to master the leg break, never easy, at the same time. After all, he had been a fast-medium bowler until a couple of years before, rather than a slow bowler who had added another weapon to his armoury.

Was Warner employing kidology in his portrayal of Bosanquet's haplessness, lest more serious hype turn to extra scrutiny ahead of greater challenges?

The summer of 1903 was one of steady progress for Bosanquet, who took 63 wickets. 'While retaining his leg break,' remarked *Wisden*, 'he had in some way acquired the power of breaking the ball from the off side without any apparent change in his delivery. This was something almost entirely new.'

MCC chose Warner to captain the England team in the following winter's Ashes, despite his having played only two Tests before. Bosanquet was also picked for the tour. Both selections concerned the press, unhappy that two such greenhorns were on the boat. Warner faced accusations of favouritism for taking his friend.

C.B. Fry, who was unable to tour, felt differently, writing an open letter to Warner, published in the *Daily Express*, 'You must persuade that Bosanquet of yours to practise, practise, practise those funny "googlies" of his till he is automatically certain of his length. That leg break of his which breaks from the off might win a Test match!'

Warner used Bosanquet sparingly in the warm-up matches, keen to maximise his shock value. When he came on his quality continued to vary, particularly his length, but Warner noticed that, against New South Wales, he 'bowled his slows very well indeed – sending down that puzzling off-breaking leg break of a good length, and continually beating the batsmen'.

Bosanquet made his debut in the first Test, at Sydney, which England won easily, taking three expensive wickets. He was dropped for the second match, another win, in which Yorkshire left-arm spinner Wilfred Rhodes took 15 wickets.

Bosanquet returned for the third Test, in Adelaide, and enjoyed some success. He got 3-95 in the first innings and 4-73 in the second, but England lost. Afterwards, Australian batsman Clem Hill made a hubristic statement, claiming, according to the media, 'Bosanquet would not get another wicket in Australia, as they had all discovered his secret.'

The fourth Test, winning which would mean England took back the Ashes after losing the 1902 series in England, confounded Hill. Bosanquet bowled only two overs in the first innings of that match, again in Sydney. In the second, as Australia chased 328 to win, his moment came. In just 15 overs of what was a timeless Test, he took 6-51. Hill, out stumped, was one of his victims. Rhodes, who had done more than anyone to get England to this position during the series, took the final wicket, but there was no doubt that Bosanquet's explosive effort had finally ensured the Ashes were England's.

The Australian press dubbed Bosanquet erratic, but acknowledged that when he got it right he was England's most destructive performer. 'How he manages to bowl his off break with apparently a leg-break action one cannot pretend to say,' said *Wisden*.

Why was that word 'googly' used? The origin is unclear, but the explanation most often accepted is that it was a combination of 'goo' and 'guile'. This merged the innocent noise made by a baby with a word denoting cunning. It fits, given the apparent innocuousness and actual deadliness of Bosanquet's tossed-up deliveries, but it sounds post-factum and contrived. Alternatively, the word might have come from the expression 'googler', meaning a high-flighted, teasing delivery. Some say it is of Maori origin.

There might be merit in this suggestion, as C.B. Fry had called it the googly, somewhat modishly, in his letter to the *Daily Express* in that summer of 1903, between Bosanquet's tour to New Zealand and Australia with Lord Hawke's XI and the following winter's Ashes. Warner said it had first been used in New Zealand too. Whatever the story, the word, sometimes spelt 'googlie', caught on.

England lost the last Test, Bosanquet not playing a major part. He could still return to England a happy man, having fulfilled Warner's match-winning expectation.

If the on-the-pitch effect of the googly was stunning, so was the wider reaction. Even though the word googly was probably coined somewhere in the southern hemisphere, its default nickname in Australia became different. Always ready to cock a snook at upper-class members of visiting England teams, barrackers had taken to calling Bosanquet 'Elsie', a tribute to the elaborate, supposedly effeminate jumpers he wore. They started calling the googly a 'Bosie'. This was apparently more than a harmless shortening of his surname.

'Bosey', spelt differently but sounding the same, was the nickname of Lord Alfred Douglas, the son of the Marquess of Queensberry, who'd had a homosexual affair with the playwright Oscar Wilde. Though never mentioned in Wilde's failed libel action against Queensberry, in 1895, and the two subsequent trials for indecency, Douglas's name was much gossiped about. The stigma of Wilde's deeds haunted English high society. His plays were removed from London theatres until several years after his death in 1900. When they returned, they were promoted with the playwright's name missing from billboards.

The Australian attitude towards Wilde was different. Even as the scandal was fresh, Sydney and Melbourne newspapers continued to mention him in reviews and gossip columns. His name appeared in theatrical advertisements in early 1896, just a few months after his imprisonment with hard labour. Whereas London regarded the idea that one of its own, albeit an anglicised Irishman, could do such things as too embarrassing to mention, the Aussies were more able to laugh them off.

The dreamer-upper of the term 'Bosie' must have known of what had happened back in London. Indeed it, like the nickname Elsie, looks to have been an earthy attempt at satire, to label the whole English ruling class as effete. Discussing the Bosie, the *Manchester Guardian*'s Neville Cardus, an expert pricker of pomposity, praised the Australian crowds' 'quick humorous sense of words and slang'. The other common term in Australia for the googly, still in use today, was a 'wrong 'un', also slang for a criminal or homosexual. Australian crowds, always ready to mock the pretensions of the supposed moral guardians of empire, wanted to make the MCC uncomfortable about its part in bringing this limp-wristed deceiver to their country.

Yet, along with mockery, Bosanquet received some 'fair dinkum' respect for his googly. After all, it had won a Test match and could do so again. An Australian newspaper remarked of Bosanquet, 'He is the worst length bowler in England and yet he is the only bowler the Australians fear.'

Bosanquet shared this explosive quality with any club leg-spinner, able to produce wicket-taking balls, but mixing them up with dross. One can understand the inconsistency. In 1897 Ranjitsinhji had remarked on the differences between amateur bowlers and professionals schooled by years of 'hard grind' and 'indispensable drudgery early in his cricket career'.

Among those watching Bosanquet's triumph in Sydney was 20-year-old Herbert Hordern. The bowler's style transfixed him, although he had to work out for himself how the effect was achieved. Displaying great intuition, he did so. Hordern managed googly reliability within a couple of years, playing some first-class matches before going to Philadelphia to study dentistry. It was not until after he returned in 1910 that he made his Test debut, becoming Australia's first international googly bowler. In just seven matches he took 46 wickets. With his mastery of length he had the control that Bosanquet had lacked.

Arthur Mailey, aged 17 when Bosanquet performed his heroics in 1903/04, saw some boys playing with a cricket ball in a park a few years later. 'One who seemed to know more than the others had learnt the trick of bowling the "bosie" or "wrong 'un",' he wrote. 'I could always bowl an ordinary leg break but this new freak ball which Bosanquet had brought to Australia mystified me. However, I cottoned on to it after a time and rushed home like somebody had found a nugget of gold.'

Mailey, born dirt poor, saw the googly as a way out. It was. He became the foremost international leg-spinner of the early 1920s. A whimsically intelligent man, he, like Bosanquet, dismissed Trumper with it, this time in a club game. 'There was no triumph in me as I watched the receding figure,' he wrote. 'I felt like a boy who had killed a dove.' Yet he had no qualms about using the googly against others throughout his career.

In England the reaction was different. After the first Test of 1907 between England and South Africa, Prebendary Wilson Carlile delivered a sermon at St Mary-at-Hill Church in London's Monument on the googly, probably related to the sins of deceit. Sadly the wording does not remain.

On a more profane level, some feared Bosanquet's delivery could corrupt cricket, rather like Wilde's homosexuality had a flower of the aristocracy. Arthur Shrewsbury of Nottinghamshire told Bosanquet, 'That ball of yours is unfair.' 'Not unfair,' he jokily replied. 'Merely immoral.'

The problem was that Bosanquet's flippant words were felt to contain some truth. To professionals like Shrewsbury cricket was a living. They wanted to protect it. There was also a sense that the Establishment had set a bad example to the Empire by using the googly to win the Ashes. It was as if natural law was under threat.

'The googly's effect was practically Copernican,' according to South African academics Richard Parry and Dale Slater. 'No longer could a batsman rely on the naïve empiricism that equated appearance and reality, what a man sees with what a man knows.'

The most outspoken critic of Bosanquet and Warner's activities was Archie MacLaren, an England captain. 'Although it may sound cowardly to say so,' he wrote as late as 1914, 'I have not participated in first-class cricket for some time because on principle I am opposed to the googly type of bowling and do not relish the stuff. The googly has certainly prevented all enterprising batsmen from playing attractive cricket, because enterprising cricket is suicidal against this type of bowling.'

MacLaren thought classical cricket – batsmen being able to play shots with certainty, at least on pristine wickets – was being undermined. His justification for his stance was that, on the uncovered pitches of the day, situations did not always favour the batsman. When rain came it sometimes created extremely difficult conditions. 'Sticky wickets' allowed traditional finger spinners – off-spinners and slow left-armers – to achieve unpredictable vertical and horizontal movement and record stunning analyses without indulging in unorthodoxy. 'It may rise with a huge break over the batsman's head,' wrote Ranjitsinhji. 'It may shoot or keep uncommonly low; it may, wonderful to relate, break from leg after receiving an emphatic off spin from the bowler's hand.' What need for anything more than orthodox bowling in such circumstances?

'Thank heaven we get wet and soft wickets, when these googly merchants are left miles behind our Jack Hearnes, Blythes, Barneses and others who keep a good length throughout,' MacLaren remarked. It was part of a quasi-religious belief, still held by many today, that cricketing luck and conditions balanced out over time. Unlike today, though, Edwardians felt nature should still have a strong, even deciding, role in a game which probably had its origins on the lumpy fields of southern England. What Bosanquet was doing was messing with the laws of chance, turning even good batting conditions into the sort of lottery that only wet pitches usually created. My view is that he was introducing more human ingenuity in to cricket, which is the whole point of sport.

Note that the word 'merchant' was being employed to describe googly bowlers. It seems harmless now, but then it had the taint of 'trade', so disliked by the upper classes. Like some seedy shopkeeper adulterating his flour with rats' bones or bartering for pennies. How odd that one of the Establishment's own number, an Old Etonian, had been credited with creating it.

'I am not afraid of the googly, and never have been,' wrote MacLaren, an Old Harrovian, 'but I consider that it kills scientific batting.' In other words, a slogger had as much chance of success. On sticky wickets, at least there was a tradition of wet-pitch excellence in batting, whereas the googly seemed impossible to decipher.

The debate over its morality rumbled on. One who saw less ill in it than MacLaren was George Gunn, the thoughtful Nottinghamshire and England batsman. Some people had 'queer notions' about it, he wrote in a debunking newspaper piece. 'They would not be surprised to see it perform a figure eight on its way to the wicket or be bowled very slow and yet reach the batsman at express speed.'

Recognising that cricket is a constant game of wits between the batsman and the bowler, and indeed between batsmen and bowlers over generations, Gunn declared that batsmen would get better at dealing with it. He was right. Jack Hobbs and others came to terms with the challenge, as leading sportsmen do. They found a way.

Some dismissed the googly as a fad, a false idol. In one report from 1909, the *Yorkshire Evening Post* described the effect of a lanky boy trying it in a match. 'He had long, thin fingers, but all the rest was the merest make-believe,' it reported. 'But he put out his tongue and made weird grimaces in the act of delivery, and bowled with exasperating slowness, and contrived to frighten some of the opposition batsmen. Their hair stood on end, their voices stuck in their jaws, and they got themselves out in wondrous ways.' Shane Warne was not the first to inspire this reaction.

Philip Vaile, best known as a tennis writer but also the author of a book on the swerve and flight of balls, related in *The Captain* magazine how England was being overtaken in a bowling arms race. There was a sense that the googly was only the beginning of a greater revolution. 'Before long it will be a raking ball with apparent leg-break action, but still with off break – in fact a fast googlie,' he wrote. More than a century later we still await that development. Pakistan's Shahid Afridi can whip them down, as did Bill O'Reilly in the 1930s and England's Doug Wright from the 1930s to the 1950s, but not at speeds one would call genuinely fast-medium or greater.

After his breakthrough in Australia, Bosanquet had his best season in 1904, taking 132 first-class wickets. *Wisden* named him a Cricketer of the Year in 1905. Australia came to England for another Ashes series that summer. It began in stunning style. In the opening match at Trent Bridge, captain Stanley Jackson hardly used Bosanquet in the first innings. In the second innings he took 8-107 in 32.4 overs, as England won by 213 runs. This was a better result than in Sydney in 1903/04, but not as good a performance.

Neville Cardus wrote that Bosanquet had sent down 'all sorts', including full tosses and balls which bounced three or four times ('polyhops' in Cardus's own phrase). Bosanquet hardly bowled again, later claiming, 'One over subsequently bowled at Harrow elicited about a quarter of a column of ribald comment in a newspaper, which finished the googly as far as I am concerned.' He made sporadic appearances for Middlesex, mainly as a batsman, during the final years of his career, ending in 1919. Like A.G. Steel, with his leg breaks and off breaks before, Bosanquet thought his work was done after a brief flourish. He had also had enough of the mockery.

Despite his successes, England picked only one other googly bowler before the First World War. Douglas Carr of Kent was almost as curious as Bosanquet. He bowled right-arm medium pace and leg breaks in Kentish club cricket, but, his imagination stirred by the googly, he decided to take it up in 1908. He quickly became good at it, playing his first match for Kent aged 37 in 1909. He succeeded and was picked for the final Test against Australia that summer. Carr took 7-282, captain Archie MacLaren putting him through 69 overs. Unlike Warner's sensitive treatment of Bosanquet in 1903/04, this mammoth spell killed the element of surprise. In its obituary of MacLaren in 1945, *Wisden* called it 'an action for which it would have been difficult to excuse anybody'.

In MacLaren's defence he had lost the toss for a fifth time in a row in the series and had precious little fast bowling on a firm wicket. Carr caused the batsmen plenty of problems on the first morning too, but it was nonetheless ridiculous. 'Mr Carr is not a young man,' *The Times* reported, 'and MacLaren perhaps kept him on too long before luncheon, and it would have been better to have kept him on for short intervals and put him on to each new batsman.' Left-hander Warren Bardsley knocked him about in scoring 136 and 130 and he lost his length a little. On an easy-paced pitch the match was drawn, Australia taking the series 2-1.

Yet *The Times* conceded that Carr had been the best of the English attack before tiring and England 'would have fared very badly without him'. It just went on too long. Was MacLaren being pig-headed in his determination to show the googly was wrong?

The situation contained a lot of what we might call 'previous'. MacLaren had a grudge against Warner. In 1903, MacLaren had written to Melbourne Cricket Club suggesting a postponement of the next Ashes tour from 1903/04 to 1904/05, as business commitments meant he would be unable to lead it until then. In response the Melbourne club requested that MCC organise the side itself instead of an individual such as MacLaren doing so, as had previously been the case. MCC agreed to this, meaning an England team would tour under its colours for the first time. It was at this point that Warner was named captain.

A peeved MacLaren leaked the information that Warner had offered to relinquish the role and tour under him. Warner denied this, saying that, in their private discussion, he had only told MacLaren he would have toured under him had he initially been named captain.

It was a silly dispute. The episode hurt MacLaren's large ego and upset Warner, a sensitive soul sometimes portrayed as a sneaky Establishment lackey. It probably coloured MacLaren's dislike for the googly, so strongly did it become associated with Warner, and Bosanquet, his team-mate at Middlesex.

Residual acrimony could have resulted in MacLaren over-bowling Carr at the Oval in 1909. Perhaps MacLaren was jealous that Warner, and not he, had noticed Bosanquet's attacking potential and won the plaudits for regaining the Ashes. If this was true, MacLaren was willing to pay an uncommonly high price for his pride. Carr had five successful seasons for Kent before fading from the scene before the First World War. There was an air of pessimism when he discussed the googly's future. 'I am quite certain of one thing,' said Carr, 'and that is that in a very short time everybody will be quite able to distinguish between the two breaks.'

While Hordern and Mailey developed their skills in Australia, and with attitudes so ambivalent in England, the centre of Empire was taught a lesson in adaptability by another outpost. In 1905/06 South Africa exposed the England batting to a barrage of googlies unequalled since. The MCC side, ironically led by a Bosanquet-less Warner, were ambushed by a quartet of practitioners – Reggie Schwarz, Ernie Vogler, Gordon White and Aubrey Faulkner – as South Africa triumphed 4-1. All four bowlers debuted in the series, making what happened more of a surprise. They managed 43 wickets between them.

The googly export was the result of Bosanquet's friendship with Middlesex colleague Schwarz, with whom he had shared his skills. Schwarz went on to tell his compatriots how it worked. It was an example of English originality being exploited and improved upon by foreigners.

The South African tourists of 1907 lost a tight series in England 1-0, thrilling crowds with their googlies. In the second Test, at Headingley, which England won, Faulkner took 9-75 in the match. England, Bosanquet, in fact, had given away the advantage of the googly. The later England bowler Ian Peebles called it the country's 'costliest export'.

When Schwarz died in the influenza epidemic after the First World War he left Bosanquet £1,000 in his will. When Bosanquet's son, a future ITN newsreader, was born in 1932, he called him Reginald.

Unlike English professionals with their packed itineraries and life of 'grind', as Ranjitsinhji had described it, the South

Africans and Australians had time to practise their skills. The British weather, making fingers and wrists stiff and cold, was seen as unhelpful too, as Wilfred Rhodes remarked after the 1909/10 tour of South Africa, when England lost again, this time 3-2. Even boys in the streets bowled it 'in a manner which is amazing to Englishmen who have tried it in vain. I fear I shall never be a success as a googly bowler. My impression is that the googly ball will always be essentially a South African accomplishment.'

Did the Blessed Wilfred, patron saint of orthodox left-arm finger spin, have a go at the googly? Delivered with the left arm, as a complement to the chinaman (going in to the right-hander), it moves away from the right-handed batsman. No left-arm bowler delivered the googly to much attention in first-class cricket until Australian Leslie 'Chuck' Fleetwood-Smith in the 1930s. What might have happened had Rhodes given it a proper go?

As late as 1922, Archie MacLaren was still banging on, saying googly bowling had gone on to 'kill the beauty of high-class batting' and was the 'root of all evil in the modern game'.

In the longer term the moral qualms were to fade, but the googly, an English invention, came to be seen as less and less English. The 'merchants' decried by MacLaren became suspicious colonials.

And, with even Wilfred Rhodes apparently struggling when he tried, the googly raised the technical standard for leg-spinners. Having a simple leg break, to be interspersed with ordinary off breaks in the way described by A.G. Steel, was no longer enough. Leg spin became harder, the potential rewards greater, the scrutiny more intense. The sweating, repressed professionals of pre-First World War England lacked the time and inclination to develop the googly, Cardus describing them as 'seldom at liberty to take the risk of a new trick, a plunge into the romantic unknown'. Meanwhile, batsmen felt threatened.

The googly, Bosie or wrong 'un remained a useful English scapegoat for cricket's ills. It could not win. Bosanquet penned a piece for *Wisden* in 1925, its tone a mixture of apology and pride. 'Poor old googly!' he wrote. 'It has been subjected to ridicule, abuse, contempt, incredulity, and survived them all.' It had been blamed for declining standards in both batting and bowling, Bosanquet complained.

He echoed George Gunn's technical clarity in his own defence. 'But, after all, what is the googly? It is merely a ball with an ordinary break produced by an extraordinary method. It is quite possible and, in fact, not difficult, to detect, and, once detected, there is no reason why it should not be treated as an ordinary break-back.' Bosanquet recognised that others had improved it, but insisted he remained a 'proud parent'.

The true parenthood of the googly is in some doubt, however. Others had done something similar, either accidentally or tentatively.

In 1906, at the height of the controversy, Bosanquet wrote that a ball behaving like the googly had been 'in common use ever since leg breaks were first invented'. So Walter Mead and others were not the first, he thought. 'Every leg-break bowler of any pretensions has frequently bowled the ball in question,' Bosanquet added, 'and owes many a wicket to it, just in the same way as every off-break bowler who gets much spin on the ball occasionally bowls a ball which breaks from leg when he is trying hard to turn it in the opposite way. The only point of distinction is that in their case the break is purely involuntary and opposite to that which was intended.'

The accolade Bosanquet chose for himself was one of intelligence. His parenthood of the delivery did not involve giving birth to it, but having the concern and stamina to nurture and care for it, to educate his own hand and those of others to produce it.

The Aussie crowds may have mocked Bosanquet, but they adopted his methods as, briefly, did the South Africans. It all goes to prove the words of the *Book of Mark*: 'A prophet is not without honour, but in his own country, and among his own kin, and in his own house.'

At a dinner in London for the visiting Australian team of 1930, hosted by Ranji, by now the Jam Sahib of Nawanagar,

Bosanquet met his greatest disciple, Australia's Clarrie Grimmett, who had taken 29 Test wickets that summer with leg breaks, top spin, googlies and flippers. Bosanquet, now 52, introduced himself by saying, 'I am responsible for you.' They chatted about bowling until the small hours.

The Barnes Ball

*'It was rather as though he had
penetrated the sound barrier.'*

Ian Peebles

THE googly enhanced leg spin. But what about speed? A.G. Steel queried the possibility of fast leg breaks. Ranjitsinhji, with help from his amanuensis C.B. Fry, noticed that bowlers like George Lohmann were able to get some movement from the off side to the leg side, known as 'action break', at pace. Rather than spinning the ball, the bowler could run his hand down the side of it in order to make the ball turn in skiddily towards the right-handed batsman – what we now call an off-cutter.

This did not work for those trying to move the ball away. 'Nothing but finger-work imparts leg break. This is the reason why there is no fast leg-break bowling. Some fast bowlers, by holding the ball loosely, can make it swing across the wicket; but this is not leg break; the ball merely "goes on with the arm" – that is, continues the direction of its previous flight instead of breaking, however slightly, from the off.'

As the 20th century got under way, someone disproved the Steel–Ranji–Fry consensus that leg breaks could not be fast. It is not flippant to call him the greatest bowler in history. Certainly the man on whom this title was bestowed was congenitally incapable of flippancy himself. His rigorously scientific approach coincided with Bosanquet's speculative experiments, but differed wildly from them. His name was Sydney Francis Barnes.

To include Barnes in a book about leg spin might feel heretically limiting. After all, he could also bowl off spin, sometimes raw pace. But the creation for which Barnes is known above all is the fast leg break which swerved in to the right-handed batsman before turning away at speed. The *Manchester Guardian*'s Neville Cardus christened the delivery – unknown before – the 'Barnes ball'.

There was no uncouth trickery, merely brilliance. Barnes, in 27 Tests, took 189 wickets at 16.43. Unlike other leg-break bowlers, before and since, he reportedly reached speeds of 70-plus mph. As a result Barnes is most often talked of as one of the triumvirate of leading 20th-century medium-pace England bowlers, the others being Sussex's Maurice Tate and Surrey's Alec Bedser. But they were primarily seam bowlers, Bedser also perfecting the 'leg-cutter', where, by dragging a finger down one side of the seam, the ball could be made to move sideways.

Barnes was a fast spinner. There had been nippy overarm off-spinners before, but there had not been genuine medium-fast overarm leg-spinners.

The 19th-century roundarm tweaker William Lillywhite was known as the 'nonpareil'. Barnes was at least as deserving of this title in his own era. Whereas Bosanquet was imitated and improved upon, this fate has not befallen Barnes, who played his last Test more than a century ago.

So, what did Barnes do? Cecil Parkin, a later England spin bowler renowned for his large bag of tricks and clowning on the pitch, summed it up well after Barnes's international career had ended. 'His length is wonderful, and he can turn the ball both ways,' he wrote. 'His best ball is almost unplayable; it is fast, and pitches on the middle and leg sticks and breaks across to the off. You dare not leave it alone because it keeps too close to the wicket. And the way he makes the ball "nip" from the turf! You would think an imp was inside the leather.'

That imp did not just leap inside one day. It took years of thoughtful practice to coax it. Barnes's story is a long and eventful one.

Born on 19 April 1873, the second of five children, in Smethwick, Staffordshire, his family played little cricket. As a teenager Barnes joined the Smethwick club, where he learned from the professional how to deliver off breaks. However, his hero was Tom Richardson, of Surrey, at the time England's best pace bowler and canonised among Oval-goers of the time for his stamina. So it was that Barnes started out his own career as a conventional fast-medium bowler. Staffordshire was then, as now, a Minor County.

Barnes came to the attention of Warwickshire, playing for them at the end of the 1894 season but not bowling. He was picked again the next year and played a few County Championship games. Nothing made him stand out as a prospect. He returned for several years to league cricket, where there was more money for less work.

Barnes played a few matches for Lancashire, where he was employed in club cricket, without success. Then he appeared in the side's last fixture of the 1901 season, a draw against Leicestershire, taking 6-70 in the first innings. Legend has it that he bowled at his captain Archie MacLaren (the same man who was so critical of Bosanquet) in the nets. 'He thumped me on the left thigh,' MacLaren told Neville Cardus. 'He hit my gloves from a length. He actually said, "Sorry, sir!" and I said, "Don't be sorry, Barnes. You're coming to Australia with me."'

And he did, to the bemusement, even horror, of the newspapers. Barnes began his first Ashes tour having taken only 13 first-class wickets. He was already 28 years old. Only £300 was on offer to professionals to tour, not enough for George Hirst and Wilfred Rhodes, who stayed at home when the Yorkshire committee offered them 'special terms' for the winter – pay to remain and keep fresh for the following summer's County Championship challenge.

An anonymous Australian press man, his nom de plume 'A Surrey Man', praised MacLaren's squad, with one caveat, 'As to Barnes, the Lancashire colt… we must give MacLaren credit for using his judgment in general, and, therefore, in this particular case his foresight may not be found wanting. This choice, however, must at present remain the mystery of the selection. Certainly as far as the writer is concerned, Barnes not having blossomed previous to the writer's departure from home in 1900.'

'Age mellows,' wrote the famously cantankerous Barnes years later. 'But in those days I was intense. I spun the skin off my fingers. I bowled with blood smearing the ball. I don't think I ever got over the questions which were asked when Archie MacLaren surprised everybody by picking me straight from Burnley in the Lancashire League for the 1901 tour of Australia. "Who is this man Barnes?" the papers asked. I determined to show them; I resolved to vindicate MacLaren. I bowled hard all the time.'

On arrival at Fremantle, Western Australia, in November, reporters asked MacLaren about the 'unknown Barnes', to which he replied, 'Well, he is well known in Lancashire… I chiefly brought Barnes because he is a real good, fast bowler, and a trundler of this class is essential.'

The team made its way to Sydney, where the newcomer was studied in the nets. 'Barnes takes full advantage of his height when bowling,' an observer said. 'He comes down in a fashion that suggests considerable danger to the batsman's wicket if he happened to be bowling on a pitch that was at all fiery or bumpy, and he can also turn the ball from the off at a very fair pace.'

Barnes made his debut in the first Test against Australia in December 1901. He opened the bowling with a fellow debutant, the Somerset leg-spinner Len Braund. In the first innings Barnes took 5-65 and in the second 1-74. Braund took 2-40 and 5-61 as England triumphed by an innings and 124 runs. Another newcomer, Kentish left-arm spinner Colin Blythe, took seven wickets in the match. The *Hobart Mercury* called Barnes's performance 'an exceptionally splendid bit of trundling on a batsman's wicket'.

After the match, a buoyant, vindicated MacLaren was interviewed, and told his critics that the bowling of Barnes, Blythe and Braund had been 'perfect'. Swiftly nicknamed 'the three Bs' in the press, they took all 20 wickets between them in about six hours.

Barnes took 13 wickets for 163 in the next Test, on a more helpful wicket, but England were thrashed by 229 runs. In the third match he had to pull out of the attack after suffering a knee injury through bowling too much. Some thought he should have soldiered on but Barnes, ever aware of his value and understandably keen to preserve the body that gave him his living, refused.

This meant a premature end to his tour. Barnes's absence in the second innings allowed Australia to chase 315 to win, losing only six wickets. 'MacLaren received many expressions of sympathy at having been deprived by an injury of his best bowler,' *The Times* reported. It might have been different had Barnes been able to bowl. All momentum gone, England lost the next two Tests to go down 4-1 in the series.

'It nearly broke my heart when his leg was strained in the third Test of the 1901/1902 rubber,' MacLaren wrote years later. 'He was easily the most versatile and difficult of all bowlers I ever had to play.'

The anguish of losing the series after such a bright start might help to explain some of MacLaren's subsequent disdain for the googly. Bernard Bosanquet was Pelham Warner's surprise pick for the 1903/04 tour. In 1901/02 Barnes had been MacLaren's. Whereas Bosanquet helped win back the Ashes, his own man had cried off at a crucial time, allowing the Ashes to slip away.

MacLaren was a deep thinker about cricket and hated it when anything, a person or an injury, interfered with his plans. He reacted angrily, with a brittleness that was sometimes self-defeating. His resentment at Warner for leading the victorious 1903/04 tour, which he had tried to delay by a year to suit himself, simmered.

In 1902 MacLaren bloody-mindedly picked Sussex off-spinner Fred Tate to play in the Ashes Test at Old Trafford, despite being angry at the selectors for including him in the squad. He seemingly wanted to demonstrate their folly to them. Tate, as has been mentioned, dropped an easy catch in the closest possible contest, helping England to concede the Ashes. His over-bowling of googly bowler Douglas Carr, a successor of Bosanquet, in 1909, despite his avowed detestation of this type of bowling, also fitted this behavioural pattern.

MacLaren lost four Ashes series as captain. Barnes in 1901/02 might have changed that. No wonder he felt so stroppy and, probably, jealous of Warner's triumph. When a player as great as Barnes is involved, on such little things as leg strains do series change.

Barnes had a voracious cricketing brain. On that tour he noticed that Australian all-rounder Monty Noble was able to swerve the ball away from the right-handed batsman at medium pace before breaking it back in. He asked Noble how he achieved this and, in a spirit of international cooperation which overcame Ashes rivalry, Noble showed him.

Swerve through the air, in the opposite direction to the way the ball is spinning, is the result of a phenomenon known as the 'Magnus effect'. It was an occurrence noted as early as the mid-17th century, when the scientist Isaac Newton, then a Cambridge University undergraduate, witnessed the strange behaviour of tennis balls hit with a spin. The 19th-century German physicist Gustav Magnus carried out further investigations, looking at lateral deviation caused by disruption of air flow across the ball. Known as swerve or drift, the ball movement through the air achieved by lateral spin is distinct from swing, which is achieved by pointing the seam in a certain direction.

Barnes wanted a practical, rather than theoretical, demonstration of the Magnus effect. Noble placed two poles on the pitch, one about halfway down and another five or six yards from the batting crease, slightly further to the off. The ball was to go to the right of the first, swerving past the left of the second. After this it broke back. This instilled in Barnes even greater accuracy and, over many hours of practice with his equally neat-minded friend, he learned what might be termed the 'Noble ball'.

Thus armed, Barnes was keen to move on and gain greater control over batsmen. But he was picked for just one Test in the following Ashes series in 1902 in England, taking 7-99 altogether before being dropped, as England looked for unlikely scapegoats for the loss at Sheffield. That was to be his last international appearance for more than five years. The idea, espoused by *Wisden*, was that he lacked an off-spinner. It was a curious suggestion, to say the least.

The story of Barnes's interaction with Noble is well known, but what about the development of the leg-breaking 'Barnes ball'? It seems something lesser was there from early on in some form but Barnes developed it, using it more frequently and with greater aplomb.

In November 1901, watching England beat Victoria before the first Test series featuring Barnes got under way, the England batsman Gilbert Jessop, part of the same touring team, wrote in the *London Evening News,* 'Barnes bowled unchanged throughout, keeping an excellent length and making the ball rise considerably. His best ball is a fast leg break.'

During the single Test Barnes played against Australia in the following series in England in 1902, the *Sporting Chronicle* stated, 'Yesterday Barnes bowled so well that the most experienced practical cricketers were astonished, and with an insidious ball which breaks away to the off he did all his damage on a plumb pitch.'

Was it a fully fledged leg break by then, though? C.B. Fry, who was playing in the match, wrote, 'He bowled beautifully, fastish-medium, almost quite fast, with a fine length, and he made the ball do just a little from the leg – not exactly a leg break, but just a trifle more than what is called "going with the arm".' Perhaps Barnes was not the finished article, according to Fry's acute, close-at-hand analysis, but something was happening, which the selectors, who dropped him (and Fry) for the fourth Test, obviously did not notice. There was indeed more than the 'going with the arm' which Fry, co-writing Ranji's book, had regarded as the maximum degree of movement to the off side possible at pace, back in 1897.

During that damp 1902 season, his first full campaign for Lancashire, Barnes took 95 first-class wickets at 21.56 and, in 1903, this improved to 131 wickets at 17.85. This was to be the last time Barnes appeared for a first-class county side. Negotiations over pay broke down and he returned to league cricket. He played no first-class matches for four years.

As googly mania swept the cricketing world, Barnes trundled on successfully in minor matches, his development little noticed. League cricket, Barnes playing at weekends and doing a proper job as in the week, allowed him more space to develop. Critics commented on a lack of stamina, but this rest from cricket gave him time to overcome injuries and be at his best for big matches in the way a centrally contracted international player would nowadays. During his lay-off from the first-class game he worked hard on his leg break.

'There can be little doubt that Barnes profits by playing comparatively little cricket, which enables him to keep fresh, and to come to each match full of energy and life,' wrote Warner, 'but for all that it is a pity he is not more often seen in first-class cricket.'

There is no known video footage of Barnes in action. Luckily some action pictures were possible. The pioneering photographer George Beldam captured Barnes at various points of his action. The *Daily Graphic* used a snap of him bowling, with Aubrey Faulkner of South Africa backing up with seemingly little keenness to get on strike, on its front page in August 1912. Barnes looks beautifully poised, his energy fully focused on the job in hand, his front leg as braced as a coaching manual would dictate. But without film there can be no indication of Barnes's 13-step run-up or the buzzing, swerving menace of the ball en route to pitching, or the spin either way off the pitch.

Yet there was a kind of honesty shown in some of the staged shots taken during his career. The bowler held the ball as he would when playing. In this regard even the stills of Barnes are extraordinary.

Unlike the usual leg-spinner, taught to cock his wrist forward to ensure the flick upon delivery brings maximum power, the seam pointing somewhere between slips and point, Barnes's wrist is quite stiff. The hand appears to be in position, as the New Zealand scientist and cricket-lover Brian Wilkins puts it, to unscrew an imaginary light bulb above him, albeit at a slightly tilted angle. The position is such that, to be able to bowl a ball in this way and achieve sideways spin using the seam, it would have to be released a fair way in front of the head.

This suggests that Barnes, like medium-fast bowlers, and unlike conventional spinners, let go of the ball in such a way as to force it downwards through the air, hitting the pitch at some speed. The largely sideways spin allowed by a stiff wrist would induce the in-drift on the ball's journey to the right-handed batsman, thanks again to the Magnus effect.

The later England bowler Ian Peebles came to the same conclusion as Barnes, that a bowler of pace who wanted to move the ball away from a right-handed batsmen appreciably off the pitch 'could only do so with any real speed by bowling the leg break in the same manner as the off break, that is without the rotation of the bent wrist'.

> The advantages of this mode are obvious, but Barnes spent some years experimenting before, as he says, it came to him quite suddenly. It was rather as though he had penetrated the sound barrier, as from then on he encountered no further difficulties, the question then resolving itself into one of refinement and application.

Because of the lack of wrist flick in the action, the spin was largely generated by finger movement. This meant only a slight change of grip, indiscernible to batsmen at the speeds Barnes reached, between the leg break and off break. The arm came over somewhere near the perpendicular for both too. Hence a degree of variation coupled with disguise that possibly no other bowler has attained. This was something Barnes worked on. 'I want to drive home that the whole run-up, action and follow-through should be the same,' he wrote. 'The arm should stay at the same height and come over in the same way.'

'My idea was to deliver the leg ball from the same height as the off,' he told the *Nottingham Evening Post* in 1935, 'thereby, instead of tossing it up, as most leg break bowlers do, to whip it down, and this, in my opinion, is the chief virtue of this particular delivery.'

Judging by pictures, Barnes also had a top-spinner bowled with an off-break action – that is, from the front of the hand, rather than with a bent wrist. This meant turning the hand round less detectably than would have been necessary with a leg-spinner's ordinary top spinner. It was probably the delivery that gained the most lift, top spin making the ball dip in the air.

Add variations of pace to all this and we begin to see why contemporaries raved about him. As the 1900s passed into the 1910s and beyond, leading players came to understand and cope with the googly. Barnes, in contrast, just got better and better.

He was recalled by MCC for the 1907/08 Ashes tour while playing for Staffordshire. The selectors were once again looking for a top-class bowler for the Ashes, with Yorkshire's George Hirst unavailable, so Barnes, who had performed marvels for Staffordshire and league sides in that county and Lancashire, was chosen. He ended up taking 24 wickets in the series. Barnes had reached near-full magnificence.

Until then he had not been seen in top-level cricket for several seasons. C.B. Fry was still puzzling over Barnes's methods in 1906. 'He is usually regarded as being able to break from leg as well as from the off, his leg break being similar to that of a slow bowler,' he wrote. 'But his leg break was not really of this kind. He had a natural power of bowling a ball which swung across from leg to the off after pitching, and he increased this by finger work so that it became something more than merely "going with the arm" and yet was not genuine break. In any case it was a very difficult ball to play.' How ironic that Fry was talking about Barnes at this stage in the past tense.

After his return to the Test scene, there was no doubt he could bowl a genuine leg break at pace. Barnes improved with age, using an action which seemed to take little out of his long body and relied on a quickness of arm. He reached 100 wickets in just 17 Tests. In the 1911/12 Ashes series he took 34 wickets, then a record for an Englishman. The superb left-armer Frank Foster took 32. Unusually today for someone able to impart spin, Barnes insisted always on taking the new ball, at one stage falling out with his captain, the equally pugnacious Johnny Douglas, when he did so instead.

With Warwickshire's Foster, Barnes formed arguably England's deadliest opening bowling partnership. Leg-spin/googly bowler Herbert Hordern played for Australia in the 1911/12 series, getting 32 wickets, but he was in no doubt about Barnes's supremacy. 'Where he was truly great was that on a perfect wicket he was just as good, in comparison, as he was on a sticky, where he was practically unplayable,' he wrote. 'Barnes, in my opinion, was the greatest bowler of all time.'

The Australian batsman Charles Macartney said of one delivery from Barnes to Victor Trumper that it was 'the sort of ball a man might see if he was dreaming or drunk'.

In the unique triangular series against Australia and South Africa in 1912 he took 39 wickets in six Tests. The pitches that summer were poor, but Aubrey Faulkner, watching as Barnes bowled an over to his South African compatriot Sibley Snooke at the Oval, gave a suggestion of the terror.

> The first ball pitched on the middle and kicked up wrist high and turned sharply away to the off. The next one came along at the right height, but the next one came back from the off and kicked. The fourth one never left the ground but was short enough to enable the batsman to play down the ball. The fifth was a good length one which hit Snooke on the jaw and stopped play for a few

minutes. The last ball was fairly respectable, only hitting him on the hand.

Faulkner, who had already migrated to England ahead of the triangular series, was in awe of Barnes throughout his life, remaining on the lookout for a world-beating fast leg-spinner to replace him when he became a celebrated coach.

Barnes's final series, England's last before the First World War, saw the then 40-year-old reach statistical heights not since beaten. Despite missing the last of the five Tests because of a row over expenses for his wife and son, he took 49 wickets – 12.25 per match. That has not been exceeded. Neither has the ranking accorded him retrospectively by the ICC. In February 1914 Barnes reached 932 points. This beat, by a single point, the next-highest total, achieved by George Lohmann in the 1890s.

In the second match of the South Africa series, Barnes took 17-159, beaten only by Jim Laker's 19-90 in 1956. 'It was Barnes's match!' recalled wicketkeeper Herbert Strudwick. 'Never have I seen anyone bowl as he did in that match. Time and again he beat the bat only to see the ball go over the top, or just miss the side of the stump.' That is quite a performance to achieve if marred by ill luck. In his final Test he took 14-144.

'Barnes dwarfed all the other bowlers... it would be hard to praise him beyond his deserts,' *Wisden* reported. 'Everyone felt before he left England that, with his remarkable finger spin, he would do well on matting wickets, but his success exceeded all expectations. He was simply irresistible.'

He played on in league cricket during the First World War and continued in this and Minor Counties matches afterwards. England, depleted by the war, sounded Barnes out about touring in 1920, but he declined, again because of a refusal to pay expenses for his wife and son. He would have reached the age of 48 while away.

He continued to eschew the googly. It would probably have damaged his arm and shoulder bowling it and, with its essential turn of the wrist, would have reduced his pace and the surprise he was able to generate with his same-seeming off breaks and leg breaks. When, in the 1930s, Don Bradman said his team-mate Bill O'Reilly must be a better bowler because he bowled the googly, Barnes responded, 'I never needed to.'

Asked in old age why no one had emulated his methods, he said, '[Alec] Bedser came nearest to me in bowling a leg break like mine. You can make batsmen, but you can't ever make a bowler.'

Barnes preached that the degree of turn from the pitch was less important than the speed at which the ball moved on bouncing. This was why he loved the new ball. Wilfred Rhodes, who himself opened the England bowling with his slow left-armers when pitch conditions were soft, was impressed. 'One thing that always surprised me about Barnes's bowling was the accuracy with which he would, with the new ball, drop a leg break of immaculate length straight away,' he said. 'Usually, of course, the new ball is a bit slippery for a spin bowler.'

Barnes's style had the extra advantage of versatility, his spin-induced swerve continuing when the ball got old. This was unlike swing bowling, then also in its infancy, which relied on maintaining shine. 'Barnes gripped the ball firmly between first and third fingers and spun it,' wrote Peebles. 'Possibly cutters have produced as good a delivery on occasions, but for consistent effect on all surfaces his method has never been equalled. The leg break was the keystone of his attack, but it was, of course, combined with every refinement of flight, change of pace, life, and accuracy... Barnes' spin was equally potent with an old ball in any weather.'

In a book I once wrote on Maurice Tate, I criticised Monty Noble for saying the Sussex medium-pacer, a heroic producer of lengthy spells on the hardest of Australian pitches during the 1924/25 Ashes, should learn more 'versatility' and 'cultivate a spin'. Tate relied on pointing the seam to achieve swing, rather than a spin-swerve. Often, because of his precision in holding the seam, it jagged unpredictably after hitting the pitch. What could be better?

Previously I thought Noble was being harsh on Tate and that to bowl genuine spin at his pace was impossible. Now I can see why he said it. Barnes was so good that even the best could learn from him. Tate had started his career as an off-spinner but switched to seam bowling, becoming the best in the world in the 1920s. Had he used Barnes's method, at least with the old ball, once the swing and seam-jag were less likely, might he have done even better? Tate was the first man to dismiss Don Bradman in Test matches, but Bradman soon learned how to handle him once the advantage of the new ball had been lost. Would Barnes have been a different prospect?

Barnes came to realise that his method was better than that of swing bowlers. 'I thought I was at a disadvantage in having to spin the ball when I could see bowlers doing the same by simply placing the ball in their hand and letting go,' he told the Australian batsman and journalist Jack Fingleton, 'but I soon learned that the advantage was with me, because, by spinning the ball, if the wicket would take spin, the ball would come back against the swing… I may say I did not bowl a ball but that I had to spin, and that is, to my way of thinking, the reason for the success I attained.'

Barnes did not just cut across categories. He created a new one: the genuinely medium-fast leg-spinner. He defied the judgement of A.G. Steel that this was impossible. He remains a one-off. The problem was that Barnes, in guarding his professional status and earning power and his naturally taciturn ways, revealed little of his *modus operandi*.

'I spun it and all my fingers did something,' he once answered when questioned about his leg break. 'I don't know how I did it myself, so how can I tell other people?' This was disingenuous, as he had spent several years attaining the control of the Barnes ball which devastated Test teams in the years before the First World War.

What went on in his mind while bowling? In interviews he was not consistent. On one occasion he said his aim was to 'always attack the stumps'. Nearly half his Test wickets were LBW or bowled, giving this some credence. But he later told that his scheming was more subtle, aiming to lure the batsman into misadventure by manipulating his movements. 'I never bowled at the wickets. I bowled at the stroke. I intended the batsman to make a stroke, then beat it. I tried to make the batsman move. The time a batsman makes a mistake is when he has to move his feet.'

As befitting a man whose countenance was described as Mephistophelean, Barnes lurked for many years in the penumbra of Minor Counties and league cricket. There was that near-recall by England in 1920. And, in 1928, aged 55, he bowled for Wales against the visiting West Indies, in the UK for their first Test series. He took 12 wickets. 'I simply couldn't guess,' said batsman George Challoner, 'as the ball floated fairly quick to the pitch, what it was going to do – leg or off spin.' The following year he took eight wickets in an innings for the Minor Counties against the South Africans.

The continuing presence of Barnes, who died, aged 94, on Boxing Day 1967, served as a reminder of the possible yet improbable. He played at a good level until into his 60s. It is estimated that in all forms of cricket he took 6,229 wickets at 8.33. This from a man who was meant to lack stamina.

The question he posed was to haunt spin and medium-pace bowlers for more than 20 years after he last played for England: How the hell do I follow that?

The Odd Couple

*'Freeman has played so rarely in Test
cricket that it is not possible to give
reasonable opinion on his qualifications
for Test cricket.'*

Herbert Sutcliffe

A S the world returned to a semblance of normality following
the First World War, a new generation of English bowlers
discussed and digested Bernard Bosanquet and Sydney
Barnes's disparate legacies.

The late 1920s and 1930s saw the most prolific burst of first-
class wicket-taking in history and a leg-spinner was responsible.
In a career lasting from 1914 to 1936, Kent's Alf 'Tich' Freeman
took 3,776 wickets, a total beaten only by slow left-armer Wilfred
Rhodes, who played the game for ten years longer. Once established
in 1920, Freeman never took fewer than 100 wickets in an English
season until he was sacked in 1936. For eight years in succession
from 1928 he took more than 200, including the all-time record of
304 in 1928. His performances included 386 hauls of five or more
wickets in an innings and 140 of ten or more in a match.

Freeman, partly because he stood just over five feet tall, tossed
up his leg breaks, top spinners and googlies, but with far more
accuracy and subtlety than Bosanquet. Known for his stamina, he
epitomised Ranji's description of a salaried bowler, going through
the 'hard grind' needed to achieve consistency.

In the years when he played, no one could worry that England lacked a top-class leg-spinner. Except they did. Freeman, despite his achievements in the domestic game, played in only 12 Test matches, while those of far lesser achievement were chosen ahead of him. Just two of Freeman's appearances were against Australia. Somehow the selectors thought of his successes as having come a little bit too easily against county tail-enders on pitches which offered easy spin. He could never prosper on the hard wickets of Australia or, indeed, anywhere against batsmen of the highest class, it was assumed. He was never picked for an Ashes match in his own country, on the pitches that supposedly suited him.

Contemporaries noticed the anomaly. 'Freeman has played so rarely in Test cricket that it is not possible to give reasonable opinion on his qualifications for Test cricket,' wrote the England and Yorkshire opener Herbert Sutcliffe. 'Judged by his record in county cricket in this country – he takes more wickets season by season than any other bowler – and with recollection of the success that has attended Australian bowlers of a similar type when they have visited this country, one is bound to say that Freeman ought to have been a valuable man for England all the time he has been such a valuable man for Kent.'

The former Lancashire and England spinner Cecil Parkin noted that 'folk are grudging in their praise of his work'. To say Freeman's successes were all against tail-enders was 'stuff and nonsense', he argued, saying, '"Tich" is a wonderful chap. There may be a lot of "rabbits" among the batsmen in first-class cricket, but there are not nearly so many as that statement suggests, neither do they always fall to the same bowler year after year.'

Freeman did not always perform alone for his county as a leg-spinner. His colleague for several years during the summer holidays was Charles 'Father' Marriott, a schoolmaster at Dulwich College, who wrote poetry in his spare time. The pair got on well but had different ideas about what leg-spin bowling should involve. They were ideas with their roots two decades earlier.

While Freeman loved to use the googly, Marriott, who had hurt his elbow while trying it as a youth, eschewed it, complaining that it could cause injuries and impede accuracy. Marriott was also of a different build to Freeman, tall and severe-looking in his uprightness.

Marriott's hero was not Bosanquet, Herbert Hordern or the South African googly quartet, but Barnes. It was ironic that Freeman, the ultimate professional in terms of matches played and overs bowled, favoured the more speculative style. But, in the amateur Marriott's mind, like that of others who had seen him at his best, the brilliance of Barnes – the most money-oriented of professionals – had ascended to a near-spiritual level.

Spending most of his boyhood in Ireland, where he attended Dublin's St Colomba's College, Marriott did not see any county cricket until he played in it, for Lancashire, in 1919, before moving south to Kent in 1922. The strongest memory of his youth was of watching Barnes bowling in Dublin in 1912. In the 1960s Marriott still glorified that day:

> I can see him now, over half a century later: the tall figure, the 12-yard run with long, easy strides, the beautiful high action with its immensely powerful body swing and follow-through, the flick of the wrist and long sinewy fingers at the moment of delivery, the perfect control of length and direction. Never again have I seen such bowling: I sat there deaf and blind to everything except the miracle unfolding before my eyes, memorising every move, my fingers itching for the feel of the seam.

He might have described Barnes as being wristier than was the case, but Marriott was probably accurate in praising his hero for not bowling a loose ball in 20 overs. 'The truth is that I had witnessed a masterpiece; after that I would never again be satisfied unless I was striving after the same kind of thing, no matter how short of it I fell.' Marriott thought deeply about the subject.

> It is the faster leg-break bowler (always provided that his length is accurate) who has the advantage against all

comers and in all conditions, for his extra pace makes it a
continual risk for even the quickest on his feet to get right
out to the pitch of the ball. I always feel thankful that I
began to realise this at school, and worked hard not only
at accuracy but at a steady increase of pace. As a result,
when I came out of the Army and went up to Cambridge,
I could bowl leg breaks at medium pace without effort.

Marriott considered the googly to be of limited use for all but
the best bowlers, in an era when the surprise over Bosanquet had
subsided. He distinguished between the 'first-rate' practitioners
and 'the rest'. 'The latter are money for old rope,' he said.

Eventually, and briefly, Marriott succumbed to the entreaties
of Freeman, who was 'so anxious that I should have a go that
to please him I did try a very few one season'. Marriott decided
to bowl one googly per innings for a few matches. Against
Leicestershire he dismissed a top-order batsman in each innings
with this method, which worked 'like magic'. Still, Marriott gave
up the googly once more, as he had done as a youth, feeling it
was not worth the extra effort and that his off break and top
spinner provided adequate variety. They had been good enough
for Barnes, after all.

Each was suited to his own brand of leg spin. Freeman,
because of his small hands, needed to use his wrist to achieve
turn. Marriott, his digits long and sinewy, was more finger-ish.
Freeman hated bowling into the wind, despite his flightier style,
so Marriott had to. He was uncomplaining, recognising his senior
partner's virtuosity.

In a book written shortly before his death in 1966, Marriott
remarked, 'The man who has at some time spun a good leg break
knows a world all of its own. It doesn't matter whether it is fast
and certain as by Barnes.' This was a false show of relativism on
Marriott's part. Nothing could ever be as good as Barnes in his
mind. He did all he could to emulate him.

In contrast, Freeman can be said to have professionalised leg-
break/googly bowling, in doing so much of it so reliably over

such a time. Bowling 1,800 overs a season was normal. He was never presumptuous about his place. He would not countenance sloppiness. 'It is beyond all contradiction that length is the chief part of bowling, and length must be commanded before any attempt at spinning the ball is begun,' he said. 'When I was coaching, I used to draw a line nine feet in front of the wicket and instruct my pupils to bowl to that; I have also laid a sheet of newspaper on the wicket and told the boys to pitch the ball on it.'

Freeman's success at county level relied on subtlety, rather than prodigious spin. Bowling so many balls a season meant preservation of muscles and bones was important. 'I have probably kidded more batsmen out than anyone,' he said after retiring. 'It may seem a strange thing to say but I got a good many wickets through not bowling the googly. The batsman knew I could bowl it and was always expecting it. Often he became so fidgety trying to watch my hand and to anticipate the googly that he got out in some other way.'

Freeman, born in 1888 in Lewisham, south-east London, started off bowling just leg breaks. In 1907, he saw South Africa's Reggie Schwarz, whom Bosanquet had taught, bowling googlies. A little like Marriott's early experience of watching Barnes, Freeman was mesmerised. 'I summoned up courage to ask him how to bowl the googly. His advice was, "Just watch me, you will soon see how it is done," and after close observation of his bowling I was optimistic enough to believe I could master it and set to work to practise bowling the googly for two years, winter and summer, before attempting it in the middle.'

Marriott and Freeman's different experiences shaped their cricketing futures. More to the point, they thought for themselves. Freeman, who claimed never to have received formal coaching, argued that true bowlers were born, not made. He also explained what might today be called his aura, the ability to play on batsmen by reputation alone. 'When you are at the top of the tree it is easier to take wickets than in the days of less experience in the art. I know I bowled better as long ago as 1914 than when I was in my supposed prime.'

This aura did not sway the selectors. Freeman made his international debut in the first Test of the 1924/25 series in Australia. His rival leg spin/googly bowler, Arthur Mailey, recalled that Australian batsmen, used to slow spinners who turned the ball more fiercely, had 'pounced upon' him. It denoted a sort of machismo ranking among leggies, those performing on the rock-hard bulli and similar soils down under having to go through a more intense apprenticeship and developing stronger wrists and fingers to get turn. This dichotomous theme continued and developed through the 20th century.

'Freeman is not a leg-break bowler, but bowls what is called a "straight break" with over spin, and sometimes bowls a ball with a suspicion of a wrong 'un,' former Australian captain Monty Noble wrote in 1925.

In his two Ashes Tests Freeman got eight wickets at 57.37 on pitches alien to him. 'He was not a success in Australia in the only two Test matches in which he played,' wrote Pelham Warner. 'I have heard, however, that fortune did not smile on him on those occasions, and that he was a great googlie bowler cannot be questioned.' Not using him in Ashes series in England, even when Don Bradman was rewriting records in 1930, was strange.

Freeman played his remaining ten Tests against South Africa and West Indies, ending up with 66 wickets at just under 26. Mailey, keen to enhance his own reputation as the top spinner of the early 1920s, remarked, 'Had he possessed skill to adapt himself to Australian conditions, no doubt he would have been ranked high among slow bowlers of all time.' He did not get much of a chance.

Marriott played one Test, against West Indies at the Oval in 1933, taking 11-96. He has the best average in Test history – 8.72 – of any bowler to have taken more than ten wickets. 'What was it but technique that enabled me,' he wrote, 'when, with trembling knees and mouth dry with excitement, I was handed the ball for my first over in a Test match, at once to strike a length and bowl a maiden to that most brilliant West Indian, George Headley, then nearing his 2,000 runs for the season?' The answer was practice. Even when unable to play because of teaching commitments,

Marriott went to the nets at Dulwich College and worked on his game.

Marriott loved the summer holidays and the chance they gave to study Freeman and leg spin in general. 'The advantage of having us both in the side was that we were so utterly different in style, pace and height. The skipper evidently thought it was well worth keeping us on together for long spells, often right through an innings. Thus every August we carried out a series of combined operations which were always intensely interesting and mostly profitable.'

Both men, in their own way, are assured of a place in history. Marriott, the enthusiastic part-timer, would be pleased with his Test match distinction. Freeman, so dominant against county opposition, would have cause to rail at his lack of representative honours. Still, he was a quiet man who did not complain publicly about injustices. Freeman's problem is that he will forever be judged against the Australian titans of his era: Mailey, Clarrie Grimmett and Bill O'Reilly.

All bowled the leg break and googly. Mailey, the first to appear in Tests, possessed huge turn and almost revelled in his lapses in length, arguing that he was always likely to take wickets.

Grimmett, who left New Zealand as a young man to pursue his dreams of becoming a world-class leg-spinner, had to move to three different Australian states before finally getting picked for Tests at the age of 33. His arm held low, he was a picture of cunning, never wanting to give anything away, perhaps because he had himself been given nothing. Grimmett used the flipper, the sort of back-spinner which floats further in the air than batsmen expect that W.G. Grace had employed in the 19th century. Grimmett flummoxed many in his era with it, but it did not create the same fuss as Bosanquet's googly before. A ball skidding on can be more effective than one coming in to the body, as Shane Warne has demonstrated with his own flippers, 'zooters', and skidders, all doused in a vat of snake oil ahead of each Ashes series. It is hard to detect such balls if bowled by an expert. They look less dramatic than googlies, but are more subtle. Grimmett was far too canny to make a fuss about what he was doing.

When he thought a batsman was able to predict his flipper because of the clicking of fingers it involved, Grimmett started clicking the fingers of his left hand while delivering an ordinary leg break.

It was scheming and deceptiveness seemingly beyond the wit of any other, although the mid-19th-century English roundarm leg-spinner Billy Buttress was said to have done something similar to make batsmen think his straight ball was a leg break, which he must have given an audible flick.

Grimmett famously used a succession of fox terriers to collect the balls he bowled in a purpose-built net in his Adelaide garden. Even in this regard his attention to detail is clear. Fox terriers are known for high energy levels and low drool output.

O'Reilly, in contrast, was all fury, his action and delivery described by Don Bradman as 'a swarm of bees'. He liberally dispensed the leg break and googly at a pace far above that of most spinners, but below that of Barnes. He came nearest to the prediction by the writer Philip Vaile earlier in the early 20th century that a fast googly would one day be possible. Growing up in the New South Wales bush, O'Reilly practised bowling against his brothers with a ball made from the chiselled-down root of a banksia, an appropriately spiky flower which thrives in Australia's arid climate.

All three Australians worked out for themselves over the years how to prosper in tough conditions. In 1924/25 Freeman had just a few weeks to acclimatise. Over time observers noticed he did not spin the ball as hard as Mailey, lacked quite the subtlety of Grimmett and certainly the hostility of O'Reilly. It is harsh indeed to compare anyone to such an amalgam of superlatives. Freeman was still a great bowler in his own right. He never got the chances he had earned.

Truly top-class, Test match-quality leg spin, one of England's many sporting gifts to the world, was seemingly becoming the preserve of another country. Grimmett and O'Reilly's Test figures in England were better than in Australia, showing that techniques learned in their harder school were portable but difficult, or impossible, to replicate through an apprenticeship in English first-class cricket.

Leg-spinners in this era were manifold at county level. Several others were tried in Tests during Freeman's career. Among them were Middlesex's Greville Stevens, Jim Sims and Jack Hearne, Nottinghamshire's Thomas 'Tich' Richmond, Derbyshire's Tommy Mitchell, Lancashire's Richard Tyldesley and Surrey's Percy Fender. Some were big characters. The former Australian captain Monty Noble, who had helped Sydney Barnes develop his swerving off break more than 20 years earlier, wrote that Tyldesley, who also bowled in the 1924/25 series, 'gives an impression of big spin, but he seems to depend more upon flight than actual break'. He thought Tyldesley occasionally attempted a googly, but it 'did not appear to be of great value'.

English leg spin was still looking fey in Australian eyes, no longer because of the eccentricity of Bosanquet's googly experiment, but because it was delivered more weakly by professional bowlers expected to get through hundreds of overs a year and unable to give the ball the same rip as Aussies who played far fewer matches.

Tich Richmond was once considered a serious rival to Freeman, but grew so fat that it was said he lost his bowling pivot. Hearne and Sims both took more than 1,500 first-class wickets. Percy Fender, who took up leg spin after watching Joe Vine bowling it in the nets at Sussex, was a top all-rounder who led Surrey, where he played for most of his career, with panache. Greville Stevens was a man of matinée idol good looks who had scored 466 in a house match as a schoolboy and became more valued for his batting than his bowling.

Neither of these observations applied to Tommy Mitchell, a miner who was discovered during the General Strike of 1926, when Derbyshire captain Guy Jackson spotted him during a match played to help rebuild industrial relations. He spun the ball a long way. Mitchell, looking a little like hapless film star Harold Lloyd in his round glasses, was a noted comedian. With this came a tendency not to take himself as seriously as some thought he should. He was talented but a little erratic.

Blatantly none was as good as Freeman.

The next big, as opposed to titchy, thing never quite happened. In one case the disappointment was especially cruel. In 1933, with England about to play their last match against the West Indies, the selectors took the unusual step of announcing all but one member of the squad. Peter Smith was watching a film in a Chelmsford cinema on the July evening before the start of the Test. An announcement came up on the screen, saying he was required outside the building. There Smith met his father in a state of excitement. He presented his son with a telegram from the Essex secretary, stating that he was to report to the Oval for Test duty the next morning.

Smith telephoned the secretary, who confirmed he was in receipt of a telegram from MCC. The next day he arrived at the Oval, where he spoke to England captain Bob Wyatt and MCC officials, who told him he had been the victim of a hoax. *Wisden* relayed that Smith had not found it 'at all funny'. It probably palled even more as Marriott, who did play, took his 11 wickets.

Still, Smith stayed for that first day as a guest of the England Board of Control. MCC secretary William Findlay was kind enough to assure him that he was good enough one day to play for England. The prophecy came true on that same ground – 13 years later. Smith featured in four Tests in total, playing twice against Australia and once against New Zealand on Wally Hammond's 1946/47 tour. His three wickets cost 106.33 each. A tilt at the weak West Indies of 1933 would have been a gentler introduction.

Lancashire's Len Wilkinson got three Tests in South Africa in 1938/39 after a flourish in late 1938, when he took 58 wickets in nine matches, aged just 21. But he lost form the following summer, partly due to a hand injury. 'The only thing I can think of,' he reminisced, 'is that I tried to be too perfect, particularly with the googly. I had an England cap and as an England player I had to be good.' The Second World War came and Wilkinson faded from the scene soon after it ended.

They all got a go at Test level. None got much of one. In terms of what they deserved, Tich Freeman got the littlest of all.

Aubrey's Dream

*'England would have had another
Sydney Barnes with which to confront
the genius of Bradman.'*

Jim Swanton

IN August 1925 a tall, 17-year-old Scot turned up at a garage in south-west London. Ian Peebles, the son of a Church of Scotland minister, was looking for adventure. He had spent a few days looking around the city before making a pilgrimage of sorts to the old garage in Richmond. This was no ordinary garage. It was the world's first permanent indoor cricket school. It had just opened, Peebles finding out about it in an advertisement in *The Cricketer* magazine, which promised to 'improve your cricket 100% in a few weeks'. He used £40 in savings gathered from his job in a bank in Edinburgh to make the trip.

As Peebles entered the tatty building on Petersham Road he was greeted by the school's owner. He limbered up and bowled in the nets. 'Although I was unaware of it at that moment, the next few minutes were to be the most important in my whole life,' he remembered.

The owner of the school was Aubrey Faulkner, one of the greatest all-rounders in cricket history. The solidly built South African was himself a very fine leg-spin and googly bowler whose greatest deeds were performed in the era of Bosanquet and Barnes, and who had been taught the googly by Bosanquet's protégé Reggie Schwarz. He watched as Peebles bowled at about medium-fast pace. Faulkner was astounded. Peebles dismissed a batsman with a delivery that reminded him of something so wondrous he had never thought it could be repeated.

'Was that a leg break?' Faulkner asked. Peebles was surprised by the question. Of course it was. The ball had hit the pitch and moved away from the batsman. Having grown up in a manse in Uddington, on the outskirts of Glasgow, far from the eyes of most English cricketing observers, Peebles was unaware of the magnitude of what he was able to do. So Faulkner, smiling, had to spell it out to him.

'I had acquired the knack of bowling the leg break at fast-medium without the orthodox bent wrist, but showing the palm of the hand to the batsman, in the manner of the great Sydney Barnes himself,' Peebles wrote.

He had always been able to do most things with the ball – spin, swing, variations of pace. But Faulkner's attentions moved Peebles's expectations on to a new level. He attended the school for more sessions. The coach, a taciturn man, became increasingly intrigued by what was happening on the matting pitches. After a few days Faulkner offered Peebles a 'most intoxicating prospect'. Would he care to leave his job at the Bank of Scotland and move south permanently to become secretary of the indoor school?

'If I did,' asked Peebles, 'do you think I would ever play for a county?'

Faulkner stood, pensively. 'If you come to me,' he replied, 'you'll go a darn sight further than that.'

Peebles returned to Scotland to explain the situation to his parents. After a while they agreed to allow him to go. Peebles started work in January 1926. So did Faulkner. He regaled Peebles with stories of what Barnes had done. 'Like most of his generation,' wrote Peebles, 'Faulkner thought Barnes was the greatest bowler of his times, and could not imagine a better in any era, past or future.'

Both boss and worker toiled in the nets, bowling at aspiring batsmen for several hours a day. When Faulkner's right arm tired, he switched to his left. Peebles developed an all-consuming relationship with cricket. He and Faulkner shared digs in Earls Court. They also came to share an obsession with emulating Barnes. Faulkner told Peebles he was the only person he had seen who could do the same things as the Staffordshire genius at the same pace.

Peebles's intense workload honed his skills so that, after a while, he could land the ball at will indoors. Plum Warner, now retired from the first-class game, was a frequent visitor to Faulkner's school and recommended him to Middlesex. 'Peebles was, at this period, one of the best young bowlers I have ever seen,' he said. 'He had everything in his favour, height, a lovely action, spin and flight.' The school transferred to larger premises in Walham Green, allowing the use of four pitches, offering different bounce and speeds to replicate a variety of conditions.

Just after he moved to London, Peebles found a book in the house he was sharing, which purported to tell people's fortunes. Perhaps it was *Gypsy Rickwood's Fortune Telling Book*, a popular publication of the 1920s, each reply reliant on the turn of a card. Barnes's question for the book he found was, 'Shall I fulfil my greatest ambition?' This was to bowl like Barnes. 'No,' said the prophet. 'The results would not be at all satisfactory.'

The book was just mumbo jumbo, but when he went outside to play matches in the summer of 1926, Peebles got a glimpse of a less than Barnesian future.

My performance was a caricature of its true potential. The pitch looked 30 yards long, the ball felt like a cake of soap, a gentle breeze became a gale, and my timing and rhythm had fallen apart. Nor did my talent ever return. I could bowl seamers, off-spinners and googlies, but the quick leg break had gone for good. Occasionally I would bowl a few fairly respectable leg breaks, but without any great life and with no lasting confidence or control. Yet back indoors I would immediately re-start where I had left off, and all our hopes would vainly rise again, to evaporate on my next appearance. It was a phenomenon Faulkner himself could not explain nor with which he could cope.

Peebles appeared to have developed a form of cricketing agoraphobia. Or perhaps it was stage fright, intense anxiety and cardiovascular activity which arises at the point of performance. By this time Peebles's expectations had risen to unrealistic levels. One of the symptoms of stage fright is sweaty palms, a feasible explanation for the apparent soapiness of the ball in his hands.

It is a feeling many leg-spinners would understand, being able to work wonders in the nets but feeling useless and exposed when called upon in a match. Yet the extremity of difference between being 'the next Barnes' one moment and a duffer the next marks Peebles out as a special case. The pressure was proving too much.

Peebles could not cope with the comparisons or the 'embarrassment' of failing to live up to the expectations of Faulkner and visitors to the school. Meanwhile, constant bowling in the nets was straining his right shoulder. Note that he was also bowling the googly. Might this hint at confusion in Faulkner's mind between the methods of Barnes and Bosanquet?

Peebles tried again and again to replicate his Barnes-like deliveries outdoors but could not. Still, Faulkner retained high hopes and, on his and Warner's recommendation, he was included in the Gentlemen's XI for the fixture against the Players at the Oval in July 1927. Still not resident in London long enough to qualify for Middlesex, it was his first-class debut. The press was quizzical to say the least. The Gentlemen v Players match, especially in a Test-free season like 1927, was the highlight of the summer.

In a dull draw, Peebles took 1-95. Yet he must have shown some promise as he was picked for the next fixture, at Folkestone in August, where he got 1-126. Similarly undistinguished performances followed in the North v South (he played for the North) and an MCC match. Still, he was picked to tour South Africa with England that winter. He got just five wickets in the Tests at 49.20, admitting he was not sure of his best style, varying between quick and slow.

Peebles, now qualified for Middlesex, left his job with Faulkner in 1928 after the two had a falling out, exacerbated by the intensity of their relationship and Faulkner's expectations.

In the summer of 1929 Peebles decided to bowl constantly at a slow-medium pace. It worked. He took 123 wickets at 19.70 runs apiece. He reasoned that this more normal method would not take so much out of him and allow him to retain control. This upset Faulkner, but Peebles proved to be extremely good at it. He bowled a mixture of conventional leg breaks and googlies.

Peebles, a suave, highly sociable man, went up to Oxford University in 1929, despite his lack of success or application previously as a pupil of the Glasgow Academy. He played for the side in 1930, leaving that year, having done almost no academic work and recording spectacularly poor exam results.

That summer saw the greatest feat of scoring in Test history, as a youthful Don Bradman remorselessly took 974 runs off England. Fresh from Bradman's record 334 at Headingley the selectors were desperate for someone to make a difference by getting rid of this growing nuisance. Tich Freeman did not get the call. Peebles was their man.

Arthur Mailey, retired as a player but working as a journalist, was rebuked by the manager of the Australian party, William Kelly, for giving Peebles advice during the Test. 'Please understand that slow bowling is an art, Mr Kelly,' he replied, 'and art is international.'

What happened in that Old Trafford match was, in bowling terms, a minor masterpiece. Rain ruined the match, but Peebles did not disappoint. In the little play possible, the pitch took turn, albeit slowly. As the journalist Jim Swanton remarked, Bradman had made all his 728 runs so far in the series in dry conditions. This was different. Peebles's first ball, a well-pitched leg break, almost bowled him. Bradman muddled on to ten, when Hammond, renowned as one of the finest slip fielders in history, missed a catch off Peebles. Soon afterwards Bradman edged another one from him and Duleepsinhji, another player who had received coaching at Faulkner's school, made the catch.

'The weather easily won the fourth Test,' *The Times* reported, 'but at least, if only temporarily, the spell of Bradman's invincibility was broken.' Bradman, not one to shower opponents with compliments, admitted Peebles had given him a 'very anxious time'. 'He bowled splendidly, and we were all in great trouble against his boseys. I frankly admitted that day I could not detect them.'

Peebles remained in the side for the final Test at the Oval. As the series was tied at 1-1, it was declared a timeless match. In Australia's only innings, Peebles took 6-204 as Bradman made a double century.

His achievement was somewhat lost amid the excitement of this innings and the fact it was Jack Hobbs's last match for England. Peebles's previous humbling of Bradman is his best remembered performance but, in statistical terms and as a show of his stamina and determination on a flat pitch, his Oval outing was superior.

However, his career, echoing the predictions of the 'clairvoyant' book he had consulted in the 1920s, declined. Peebles, even in 1930, was losing the ability to turn his leg break, he and others blaming his overuse of the googly. 'It was significant that one of the few leg breaks he bowled in the Test matches proved the means of getting rid of Bradman,' *Wisden* commented.

Peebles had two excellent series against South Africa and New Zealand in 1930/31 and in 1931, taking 31 wickets in total. But his shoulder broke down at the end of 1931, ending his Test career at the age of 23. He continued to play for Middlesex until 1948, despite losing an eye in a Second World War bombing raid.

The sense of genius lost remained. 'Perhaps he went to South Africa at too young an age; perhaps he played too much cricket, and certainly he was overworked to a horrible extent at Faulkner's School,' wrote Warner, 'but no-one could have bowled much better than he did in the Test Match at Old Trafford.'

Mailey felt deep disappointment at Peebles's decline. He had taken a course in ballistics to understand better what the ball was doing and enjoyed discussions with Peebles on the subject, remarking that 'and yet I could never understand why one so far up in technical knowledge of flight variation could lose his leg break, particularly in the thirties, when England were looking for a good slow bowler. Although I was an enemy in England's camp then, I shall never forgive Ian for that lapse.'

It was not a decline Faulkner lived to see. During that Old Trafford match of 1930, Peebles was returning to the team hotel in a taxi when he spotted Faulkner, who was working as a radio broadcaster, waiting in a bus queue. He got the driver to stop and gave him a lift. The two exchanged pleasantries and discussed old times in the bar of the Midland Hotel. It was the last time they saw each other.

On 10 September 1930, less than seven weeks after Peebles had made Bradman look a mug, Faulkner committed suicide. He stuck his head in the oven in the small bat factory adjoining the cricket school. His secretary, Ronald MacKenzie, smelt gas and summoned a policeman. The pair found Faulkner with his mouth over a gas jet. He had left a note saying, 'I am off to another sphere via the small bat-drying room. Better call in a policeman to do the investigating.'

Faulkner and his new, young wife Alice had been planning a trip to Paris a week later. At the inquest she said he had once previously threatened to take his life by gassing himself but usually his depressive episodes had sorted themselves out when he went out on his own for a walk.

'He used to enjoy good health, but at the end of last year he was not so well,' she said. 'I think he had overworked a great deal, and he had two operations, which left him far from well.' He had been 'very temperamental', she added. The inquest in Fulham recorded a verdict of suicide while of unsound mind.

Faulkner was a man of many acquaintances but few close friends, but his death at the age of 48 shocked the cricket world, Peebles included. 'When I went to call on his young widow she told me something which moved me profoundly,' he wrote. 'When he seemed to lose heart and all taste for life, she said, he had one abiding interest. It was to look in the morning paper to see how many wickets I, his discovery and protégé, had taken the previous day.'

The journalist and broadcaster Jim Swanton, a friend of Peebles who shared a flat with him in the Temple area of central London after he left Oxford, described Faulkner's sense of pride mixed with regret at the way Peebles had done things. 'Peebles was to bowl successfully in many Test matches... but Faulkner, one of the greatest judges of a cricketer that ever lived, used often to maintain that if only he could have produced in the open the form he showed indoors, before he had been heard of, England would have had another Sydney Barnes with which to confront the genius of Bradman.'

Faulkner was a man with demons. He had grown up in Port Elizabeth in a home dominated by his alcoholic father, Frank, who beat up his mother, Anne. When he was 15, he returned from cricket practice one day to find Frank drunk and attacking Anne. By now a thick-set young man, he hit his father so hard that he knocked him out of his shoes. It must have been a wretched upbringing. As a result of his disgust at Frank's boozing, Faulkner became a lifelong teetotaller. The cricket school was not experiencing financial problems when he died, but a fund-raising deal had fallen through and Faulkner refused to open a bar there on a matter of principle, reducing his potential profits.

He served with distinction in the First World War, seeing action in Salonika, Egypt and Palestine, reaching the rank of major and winning the Order of the Nile. But he caught malaria. In the advert for his cricket school, published just after it opened in 1925, Faulkner urged young cricketers to 'place yourselves in the hands of one who has been through the cricketing mill'. Not just cricketing. He'd had a lot to deal with in his life and, at its end, Faulkner could not shake off his depression.

At the inquest, the coroner said Faulkner's suicide note had included a few other words which did 'not matter'. These can only be a matter of conjecture, but usually coroners keep such details under wraps to avoid hurting the living.

Faulkner's problems ran deeper than cricket, but might the situation with Peebles – his failure to live up to the impossibly high standards of Barnes – have contributed to his state of mind, or at least acted as a point of fixation? Might Faulkner have referred to this in his suicide note? We can never know.

What we can say is that much of Faulkner's time was taken up with trying to develop something like Barnes. Peebles continued to share Faulkner's belief in Barnes as an ideal to emulate, as late as 1968 writing of him in *The Cricketer*:

> No one before (so far as one can ascertain) or since has been able to utilise his technique although it was logical and simple, for basically it consisted in bowling the leg break in the least complicated way, which is to say like the off break, from the front of the hand. Without the elaborate bend and turn of the wrist the ball can be more simply controlled, and bowled at very much greater pace. All this is perfectly clear in theory yet Barnes has had no outstanding imitator, nor successor.

Cricket writers and schoolboys often speculate on how the best bowler of one era would fare against the best batsman of another. Barnes and Bradman were arguably the best of any era. Faulkner, who watched much of Bradman's run-scoring while working as a broadcaster in 1930, must have come to feel he had almost facilitated such a contest between the two, with Peebles as proxy for Barnes. That morning at Old Trafford was good but, because of Peebles's troubles and the fact that he had changed his style from the Barnesian to the conventional to achieve it, not quite good enough for Faulkner.

Barnes did not disappear, becoming just a semi-imaginary figure from the past. His last first-class match, for Wales against MCC at Lord's, ended on 22 August 1930. On the same day, on the other side of London at the Oval, Australia won the Ashes. Peebles was the not out batsman as Wally Hammond was dismissed to finish the match. Bradman never faced Barnes in first-class cricket.

Faulkner did not just teach leg spin, of course. Sussex and England's Duleepsinhji, in that summer of 1930, scored 173 in the Lord's Test, still reckoned to be one of the best innings in that ongoing contest.

Faulkner wanted to buck the English system of over-grooming players, of making them perform within prescribed limits, saying he based his system upon 'a collection of "do's", rather than on one of "don'ts"'. He also claimed never to tell a player what to do without explaining why. English coaches were often 'lazy in mind', he reasoned, and, 'When the hapless old methods fail to produce cricketers, it is maddening to hear that it is the boys, forsooth, who are to blame, and not their mentors. Ye gods! We coaches, I fear, are indeed a self-complacent lot.' Plum Warner, for one, felt Faulkner's philosophy was likely to have a profound effect on English coaching.

He could teach anything, but leg spin was his pet subject. Bowlers needed 'to look a little further than to length pure and simple'. It was important to teach more than 'the wearisome and monotonous length that reduces so many county games to such boring affairs'.

If Faulkner noticed a boy had the 'propensity to spin the ball from leg I encourage him to persevere with his spin – and help him at the same time to gain length. I would never dream of making a young fellow sacrifice, in the beginning, spin for length... The boy that can make the ball do a little naturally is far too valuable a product to kill by pumping blind length into him.'

He argued that it was part of a coach's job to know 'precisely when to rest' a young player. In that regard Faulkner summarily failed with Peebles, whose shoulder experienced far too much wear and tear as a teenager to allow him full effectiveness over a long career.

Barnes and Peebles met on several occasions. On one, at Lord's in 1930, the old master showed the younger man his technique. Peebles called this 'a glimpse of the bowler's promised land'.

Peebles, an aspiring journalist, wrote about one conversation in the press, but was embarrassed when the report was published with a headline that made Barnes furious. 'It was a pity that an enterprising sub-editor had captioned the account, "Barnes tells young bowler how he would get Bradman out". He was furious at being put in this false light, and it took Sir Pelham's advocacy to convince him that I was naïve, but certainly not guilty.' It was hardly the most incendiary headline in newspaper history, but Barnes was apparently angry at being portrayed as arrogant. He could still bristle with the best of them.

The experience did not deter Peebles from the world of print. He became a wine trader and part-time journalist, his respected articles and books informing cricketing debate until the early 1980s, when he died of cancer. Peebles's son Alastair, who followed his father into the drinks trade by running a wine-tasting school in Devon, remembers a 'marvellous' man. Peebles's genial good nature meant he retained friendships within the game. In his writings he mused about his shoulder injury, but not in conversation. 'I think it was very frustrating for him, but he never really discussed that with me,' says Alastair. 'He would say he had had a very good life. For the son of a minister he got a long way. He was a man without side.'

Peebles remained philosophical. He summed up his career well. 'I was a good might-have-been, or maybe a might-have-been great,' he wrote.

What of Faulkner's other charges? Before he started his indoor cricket school he taught at St Piran's prep school in Maidenhead, Berkshire. One of his pupils was Freddie Brown, a Peruvian-born future Surrey and Northamptonshire player who captained England on the 1950/51 Ashes tour. He retained respect for 'the Major', attending his cricket school.

Brown spent the Easter holidays of 1930 with Faulkner, ahead of going to Cambridge later that year. 'It was during this period that he changed me from a new-ball medium-pace bowler – with an occasional leg break – into a leg-breaker with an occasional quick one,' he remembered. 'He argued that the competition for a place in the Cambridge side as a leg-spinner would not be so keen – and most grateful I was to him for what he did.'

Brown, who was a prisoner of war from 1942 to 1945, having been captured at Tobruk, became known as a martinet as captain. He revoked his leg-spinning for medium pace for a while during the 1950/51 Ashes tour, reasoning that it would be pointless on the unforgiving pitches encountered.

Another of the visitors to the Faulkner School of Cricket was Walter Robins who, like Peebles, played for many years for Middlesex and appeared in Tests. Educated at Highgate School and small and wiry of build, he was a teenage prodigy at football and cricket. Faulkner developed him as a leg-spin bowler. *Wisden* noted that he 'could not always command a good length; but though he sometimes came in for punishment he was always capable of producing a telling delivery'.

Peebles described the Robins of the late 1920s as the 'best English leg-tweaker I ever saw'. Disdainful of flight, he whipped down leg breaks and googlies at a pace well above that of most spinners. Robins was a brilliant fielder and had a low boredom threshold and extrovert personality, believing in cricket as entertainment. 'He bowled at a great pace, and his beautiful action and body swing would have satisfied the most severe critic,' wrote Plum Warner. 'He seemed to "spit fire".'

His greatest dismissal, among the 64 he achieved in 19 Tests, was Bradman bowled by a googly for 131 in the second innings of the Trent Bridge match in 1930. Bradman did not even offer a stroke. The pair, who were good friends, used to argue affectionately over the incident for years.

'Don always used to say to me, "Oh, I meant to get out to your father",' says Robins's son Richard, also Bradman's godson.

'I said, "Come on, Don, of course you didn't. You never gave up anything in your life."

'He said, "I know he wanted to marry that girl, you know. The only way she would give up was if I got out to him."'

Robins did indeed marry Kathleen, one of the spectators that day. The idea Bradman would show such largesse during a run chase which ended up with England victorious by 93 runs is fanciful. Robins effectively won the match with a ball of brilliance.

But he could be inaccurate. 'It is agreed that a leg-spin bowler is needed to dislodge Bradman,' wrote Neville Cardus in the *Manchester Guardian* in the summer of 1932, while the side to go to Australia the following winter was under discussion. 'Probably Robins and Brown would be useful if they would bowl good-length balls more than three or four times a week.'

A coach, seemingly in contradiction of Faulkner, prevailed upon Robins to slow down in pursuit of control. By general consent this made him less effective.

Robins remained a major force in cricket as an administrator and manager until his death, at the age of 62, in 1968. Another reason for his place in cricketing folklore was the bestowing of the name 'chinaman' on the left-armer's version of the leg break, a delivery that turns in to the right-handed batsman. The story goes that Robins was facing Ellis 'Puss' Achong, a bowler of oriental descent, delivering the ball in this style, in the Old Trafford Test of 1933. After he was stumped, he reportedly said, 'Fancy being bowled by a bloody Chinaman.' West Indies all-rounder Learie Constantine then supposedly inquired whether Robins was referring to the bowler or the type of delivery and the name stuck.

Richard Robins says his father, a lover of fuss of any kind, whether born of adulation or notoriety, was happy to be associated with the tale. But, he adds, he told him it was not true and that fellow England batsman Patsy Hendren had made the comments, using a word slightly ruder than 'bloody'. This is possible, especially the sense of surprise at the type of delivery, as Achong bowled Hendren for 77 in his debut Test at Port-of-Spain, Trinidad, in 1930.

Robins played sporadically in first-class cricket until 1958, taking 969 wickets at 23.30. Faulkner never saw most of it, but he would have been proud. Still, he got to see two of his leggies play for England and dismiss Bradman.

Robins and Peebles played in a Middlesex side seemingly obsessed by leg spin. Even the South African quartet of the 1900s paled numerically as the county side on occasions in 1930 included five England leg-spinners. Jack Hearne, Greville Stevens and Jim Sims played alongside Peebles and Robins. The South African Test leg-spinner 'Tuppy' Owen-Smith, who played rugby union for England, also turned out for the side from 1935 to 1937.

The Faulkner-taught bowler who achieved most in international cricket was Doug Wright. Born in Sidcup, Kent, just a few days after Britain entered the First World War, he left school aged 15 in 1930 to become a legal clerk but in the summer managed a few matches for Chislehurst. While there, Gerald Simpson, captain of Kent's second XI, noticed some potential and recommended him to Faulkner.

Faulkner offered Wright a job on his coaching staff, saying, 'Work with me and I'll teach you how to play cricket.' Wright, quiet and eager to learn, spent hours discussing the theories of leg-spin and googly bowling. Faulkner offered Wright some simple advice, 'Keep it up to the bat.'

Unfortunately his most venomous-looking deliveries had the habit of pitching several feet too short. So, unlike Peebles, Wright decided to bowl quicker and with a flatter trajectory. This worked. Wright's success with this method was not restricted to the nets. Unlike his predecessor at Faulkner's school, he could replicate the fast leg break, albeit a wristy, orthodox ball rather than the stiff-wristed Barnes type, outdoors.

Kent were delighted with the results and offered him a contract. In 1932 Tich Freeman missed a few matches and Wright made his debut. He made steady progress over the next few years, Freeman always ready to offer advice. It was the same as he had given to Father Marriott.

'When Warwickshire were playing Kent at Gravesend in the first year Douglas Wright turned out for us,' Freeman remembered, 'I got a wicket with the last ball of an over and (Leonard) Bates came in to take the next ball from Wright. I suggested to Wright he should bowl a googly first ball; he did and Bates's leg peg went down. Bates said to me afterwards, "You told him, Tich, didn't you, to bowl a googly?" and I admitted the little strategy.'

Wright's breakthrough came in 1937, the year after Freeman was sacked for getting 'only' 110 wickets. Wright took 111 wickets in 1937, followed by 110 the next. During his career, which lasted until 1957, Wright took more than 2,000 first-class wickets. In Tests he became England's most successful out-and-out leg-spinner in terms of wickets. Barnes could not be included in this specific category, such was his variety of weapons.

Wright's long run-up was one of the more bizarre in history. 'His approach looked like a cross between a barn dance and a delivery stride,' according to the Australian writer Ray Robinson.

'D.V.P. Wright of Kent is a manifest basket of talent,' wrote C.B. Fry in 1946. 'He is called a "leg-breaker", isn't he? And on his day he bowls the leg break at a pace faster than the usual bowler of this sort well enough to run through any side. On other days he seems to bowl with the limit of ill-luck.' He saw Wright as a sort of missing half of the perfect bowler, the other being off-spinner and off-cutter George Lohmann of the late 19th century. 'If George Lohmann had had command of Wright's leg breaks, as well as of his other artistry, he would have been even more formidable than he was. Vice-versa applies to Wright.' That was quite a compliment.

One of Peebles's successors as an employee of Faulkner's school, Tommy Reddick, was reckoned to be a talented leg-spinner/googly bowler in his youth. He later focused on his batting, playing for Middlesex and Nottinghamshire before moving to South Africa. He became a respected coach and journalist.

Stan Squires, like Peebles fleeing life at the bank a few years earlier, gave up work in a stockbroker's office to pursue his dream of becoming a first-class player. He joined Surrey in 1928 and remained there until 1949. His bowling career is intriguing. 'As a slow bowler he specialised in off breaks, although in later years to suit his county's needs he turned to the leg variety,' Wisden said in its obituary after he died in 1950, aged just 40, from a blood disease.

After the Second World War, off-spinner Jim Laker was in the Surrey team, as was Alec Bedser's twin brother Eric, who bowled in the same style, necessitating Squires's move to leg spin. This seemed to set his mind working. Squires cross-fertilised the off break and leg break in a way even Bosanquet had not imagined. Laker left an enticing tale:

> Stan was the only man I knew who could bowl the 'inverse' leg break with an off-break action. It was the perfectly disguised ball, and Stan would often amuse himself and confuse others by bowling it out in the middle in between the fall of wickets. But he could only bowl it from a standing position, not with a run-up, and he never attempted it in a match.

This sounds like the ball popularised by, and often attributed to, Pakistan's Saqlain Mushtaq in the 1990s, known as the 'doosra', meaning 'second' or 'other' in Hindi and Urdu. So Squires, a man taught by Faulkner, himself a friend of googly expert Reggie Schwarz, who had learned the trick from Bosanquet, had himself done something apparently new.

It has a glorious symmetry – sort of literally. Events started by the populariser of the googly might have seen the doosra created in England, via the involvement of two cerebral South Africans.

Although Squires never dared try his invention in a match, he pushed at cricketing boundaries in the way that Barnes and his admirer Faulkner had encouraged. Sadly Faulkner, the coach who had given so much of himself, found no happiness in this 'sphere'.

Even so, Peebles, Brown, Wright and Robins took 258 Test wickets between them. What more might Faulkner have achieved had he lived longer?

Eric's Saga

*'It is not their fault that great leg-spin
bowlers are not bred in a land where rain, or
some sort of moisture, is always encouraging
an easier way of obtaining wickets.'*

Neville Cardus on England selectors

NO English leg-spinner of the 1920s and 1930s cemented
a place in the team the way Australia's Arthur Mailey,
Clarrie Grimmett and Bill O'Reilly did. One man, other
than Tich Freeman and Ian Peebles, who might have done was Eric
Hollies. Born in the Black Country in 1912, he learned cricket,
according to his own romanticised account, on pit mounds. House
bricks served as stumps. The compacted coal remains that gave
the area its name became true, fast pitches for boys.

Hollies's father was a leg-spinner who injured his arm as a
young man and continued to bowl underarm. Hollies senior
passed on the overarm technique to his son. Eric's sister learned
too, in what was a family hothouse of leg spin. 'Before he
introduced me to that fundamental matter of "ABC", he made
sure I could bowl a decent-length leg break,' Hollies wrote.

By the age of eight he could do this passably well. A year later
he had evidently progressed. The nine-year-old bowled in an
impromptu game outside a hotel in Rhyl, North Wales, where
his family was on holiday. A resident wandered into the lounge
and asked, 'Does that fair boy belong to anyone here?'

'Are, that 'ud be my lad,' replied Hollies's father.

'Well, do you know he's bowling googlies, and at his age, too?' the fellow guest added.

Hollies kept practising and joined Old Hill in the Birmingham League. He left school at the first opportunity, worked in the family plumbing business for a while and almost signed for Worcestershire but, because of an administrative mix-up, was not offered terms. Instead, in 1931, he joined Warwickshire where, for more than two decades, he became as much a fixture of the Birmingham scene as canals.

The groundsman at Edgbaston was Ted Leyland, father of Yorkshire and England batsman Maurice Leyland. Ted was a former league-standard leg-spinner who took time to talk to Hollies about variations of length, flight and pace and how to use the googly to the best tactical advantage.

In his early days on the staff he felt inferior to a rival leg-spinner called Harry Jarrett, who, he reported, could spin the ball more than Tich Freeman and was faster through the air than Doug Wright. At least he could do so in the nets. When out on the pitch Jarrett was a bag of nerves. It was reminiscent of Ian Peebles's early travails when emerging from Aubrey Faulkner's indoor school. Hollies was made of more stoical stuff than Jarrett and impressed with his performances in minor matches.

He made his first-class debut in 1932 against Sussex. His third game, against Kent at Birmingham's Mitchells and Butlers' Ground, was also the debut of Doug Wright. Their two careers were set to run in parallel, becoming 'great rivals', in Hollies's words. Had they been Australian, like Clarrie Grimmett and Bill O'Reilly, they might have become a great partnership.

In the winter of 1932/33 Hollies joined a 'physical culture class'. Hours of bodybuilding and stamina work gave the sandy-haired, squat 20-year-old the physique to cope with long spells.

Another Hollies characteristic that stood out was his accuracy. Starting off at above average pace, he was never a wristy type who gave the ball a huge rip as he released it. Rather he was described by contemporaries as a 'finger spinner'. He got just enough spin either way and was able to keep the best batsmen pegged down.

This stemmed partly from an early introduction to the realities of first-class cricket from Wally Hammond, second only to Don Bradman among batsmen of the 1930s. In his fourth match for Warwickshire, Hammond belted Hollies around Gloucester's Wagon Works Ground for 57 off six overs. From then on he promised himself he would be more pragmatic and less flighty.

Hollies came under the influence of county captain Bob Wyatt, who had also led England. He was not universally liked, a cool thinker rather than a warm man. Yet his advice on field placements and remaining calm were invaluable to Hollies. 'Collectively it represented the basic knowledge so vital to a bowler with hopes of making a career in county cricket.' In one match Wyatt told Hollies that Middlesex and England legend Patsy Hendren was 'an ordinary' man. His nerves calmed, he dismissed him twice. Hollies played three Tests in the West Indies in early 1935. He took ten wickets at 21.70.

However, the following summer was to prove farcical for English leg spin. The Lord's pitch for the second Test against South Africa was in a terrible condition. It had become infested with crane flies, known as leatherjackets. They created bald patches, which meant the pitch provided unexpected amounts of turn during the season. A wristy leg-spinner, unlike Hollies, was felt to be necessary to exploit the conditions and the selectors discussed the matter in detail.

Pelham Warner and most of the committee wanted Walter Robins of Middlesex. Captain Bob Wyatt insisted on Tommy Mitchell of Derbyshire, in form that summer. Wyatt's view prevailed and Mitchell was picked. Warner's biographer, Lawrence Meynell, wrote 'that they were unwise to agree to the inclusion of Mitchell as the records, if anyone chooses to look them up, will show'.

Mitchell took 3-164 in a match won by South Africa, their first victory in England. *The Times* reported that Mitchell had been 'so inaccurate that his captain could scarcely have dared to put him on. It is bad not to be able to employ one's leg-break bowler.'

What made it worse was that the visitors' own leg-spinner, Xenophon Balaskas, took 9-103. Arthur Mailey thought Mitchell a good bowler but 'out of his class when the heat was on'.

Hollies was picked instead for the next Test at Headingley, traditionally not a big-turning ground. He added to the farce. During Warwickshire's match against Glamorgan at Swansea he injured his neck one night when a team-mate stumbled into his bedroom without turning on the lights and fell on him. At least, that was his story. The selectors wondered whether irresponsible high jinks, maybe fighting, were to blame. One of them, Pelham Warner, later wrote that he had 'had his neck wrung in a playful scrap'.

Whatever the reason, Hollies did not turn up at Headingley, instead going for treatment in Birmingham, and claimed the selectors had held a grudge against him thereafter. Jim Sims of Middlesex played instead, taking 1-68.

Mailey thought Hollies and Mitchell both lacked the 'tenacious stubbornness' for Tests. It may have been harsh, but the summer of 1935 did neither any good. The name of English leg spin was not well served either. Greater historical forces have damaged it over the last century, but this does not mean individuals' failings bear no blame whatsoever.

Until the war broke out in 1939 Hollies whirred along at about 100 wickets a season. His relationship with England remained fraught. He was angry not to make the 1936/37 Ashes tour after captain Gubby Allen allegedly told him he would be going. Sims and Robins went instead, underwhelming judges.

Neville Cardus regretted the selections made, as O'Reilly took 25 wickets for Australia. 'Leg spin would have come as a boon and a blessing to Allen,' he wrote, 'but, truth to say, there is not in English cricket at the moment a single leg-spin bowler of Australian ability. English wickets encourage conventional pace, new ball shibboleths and the finger spin of a hoary tradition.'

'But it was foolhardy of England to take the field without leg spin' in one match, he averred in another report, 'even the leg spin of Sims, which often remains an idea in the mind of Sims.'

Cecil Parkin, the multi-faceted spinner and arch-joker of the 1920s, offered a novel explanation for the non-success down under. Australian spinners, he said, had the advantage of being 'used to the terrific heat; whereas the Englishman perspires a great deal while playing and cannot therefore spin the ball to the extent that he can in this country. The ball slips in his fingers, and it is only towards the end of the tour that the English spin bowler finds himself at his best, through becoming acclimatised.'

Sweat stopped Englishmen spinning, he reasoned. Perhaps Clarrie Grimmett, with his experience of bowling with a ball brought to him from the other end of a net by a dog, even had an advantage with the wet ball! But English bowlers should have been able to cope with dampness, given the conditions at home.

Hollies missed the 1937/38 tour to India with Lionel Tennyson's XI, after Warwickshire recommended he stay at home and rest. That was it for the time being. His greatest moment, possibly the most famous single event in cricketing history, was to come years later.

Officials Attack

*'The rules have been so senselessly
directed towards speed and swing that
no thoughtful young bowling aspirant
would deem it worth his while to even
think of concentrating upon leg spin.'*

Bill O'Reilly

I N 1935 England's administrators launched what some saw
as an unprovoked attack on leg spin. They changed the leg-
before-wicket legislation. Previously an appeal could only
succeed if the ball pitched in line between wicket and wicket.
Now, for an experimental period in England only, batsmen could
be out if the ball pitched outside off stump, as long as it struck
the pads in line with the stumps and was going on to hit them.

This, according to the Association of Cricket Statisticians,
saw the proportion of LBW dismissals in County Championship
matches rise from 13.5 per cent in the period from 1931 to 1934
to 17.8 per cent in 1935. It subsided a little thereafter, but the
indignation remained.

Surely the LBW change would negate leg spin, which moves
away from the right-hander, by giving off spin and in-swing a
greater chance of success?

Remember 1935 was also the year when Eric Hollies, by his
absence from the Headingley Test, and Tommy Mitchell, by his

inaccuracy on a helpful pitch at Lord's, were deemed to have let England down. It was a bad, bad season for leg spin.

One who unsurprisingly thought this was Bill O'Reilly, who had taken 28 wickets in the 1934 Ashes. Decades later he still seethed about the English authorities. 'They have tried time and again to handicap leg spin out of the game. Why did they think it necessary to try to destroy leg-spinning in the mid-1930s by introducing the infamous LBW rule which meant that a batsman could not be given out LBW if the ball pitched outside the leg stump?'

O'Reilly's description of a vendetta is a touch misleading. The authorities had not legislated to make things harder for leg-spinners like him. They had merely given greater help to other types of bowlers. Of course, there was also a greater chance of getting a wicket with the googly now too. But, by distributing largesse elsewhere, to off-spinners and in-swingers, the result was likely to discourage people from a harder path of leg spin. The whole idea had been to stop some of the huge scoring which went on during the 1920s and 1930s. It was intended to create more 'brighter cricket', at least in terms of matches ending in positive results. How misguided it was.

The revised LBW experimental law was tested for two seasons in England before being adopted permanently in England and Australia in time for the 1936/37 Ashes. There is an argument that its effect would be harder felt by leg-spinners in England, where the ball tended to bounce lower and LBW was a more common mode of dismissal.

There was some discussion of extending the LBW change further, so that balls that pitched outside the leg stump and hit the pad in front of stumps could count. O'Reilly would have liked that, but the thought failed to gain traction. Hollies was one of those opposed, worrying about 'a rush' of LBW-aimed leg-break bowling. There was more to it than that, surely.

Leg-spinners went off to war a little disgruntled about the injustice heaped upon them, but, as the afterglow of victory over Hitler abated, an act of vandalism took place.

For 1946, MCC decreed that in matches in England a new ball should be made available every 55 overs. The shine would barely be gone before another became available. It was strange indeed at a time when leather, rationed because of the huge demand to make soldiers' boots and jackets, was in short supply. By the end of the war, the amount allowed equated to two pairs of shoes a year per person. There was a boom in sandal sales as fashion-conscious women tried to make their allotment stretch further.

MCC was evidently not as materially thrifty, stating, 'After 55 overs (six balls) have been bowled with a ball in such matches, the fielding side can demand a new one, when the umpire shall inform the batsmen of the change. (In 1946, in the event of a shortage of balls for any match, before the commencement of the match the captains may mutually agree to apply this experimental rule to the substitution of selected old balls in sound condition.)'

It devised a system of warnings for teams and spectators. 'After the 45th over, the scorers shall display a small white flag or signal, which shall be replaced by a yellow signal after the 50th over. At the commencement of the 55th over both signals shall be exposed.'

Raising the white flag was an appropriate metaphor for what happened, as far as leg-spinners were concerned. Unless one was S.F. Barnes, gripping a new ball was difficult. The change put a further premium on easier-to-control trundle. Arthur Mailey was not pleased, calling the 55-over rule 'crazy'. 'Unless he can reach the heights of Maurice Tate or Alec Bedser,' he wrote in militant indignation, 'there should be no place for the medium-pace bowler in big cricket.'

Mailey was a purist, but the more pragmatic Don Bradman also thought the new-ball stipulation 'had the effect of pushing the leg-break bowler somewhat into the background. Captains thought it safer to bowl tight in between new balls and let the damage be done by the fast men. This in turn reduced scoring rates, and a leg-spinner dearly loves to have a few runs to play with to give of his best.'

Why did it happen? O'Reilly, an anti-imperialist proud of his Irish ancestry, had a point of view:

> The answer is simple: the English were sick to death of leg spin, and well they might have been. They could not handle it, so they decided to destroy it. They did that with such comprehensive success that the art of leg-spinning is in danger of disappearing from the game.
>
> The changed rules have been so senselessly directed towards speed and swing that no thoughtful young bowling aspirant would deem it worth his while to even think of concentrating upon leg spin, and I have heard it said that modern captains dare not use leg-spinners for fear they might lose a match in three or four overs of big hitting.

For the 1949 season the new ball was to be taken every 65 overs in county cricket and, by the late 1950s, this was raised to 75 overs. For the 1961 season, the Advisory County Cricket Committee increased this once more to 85 overs, after county captains agreed unanimously to provide 'entertaining cricket during the coming season', amid concerns over turgid play and declining attendances. It was too late for leg spin. Negativity was by now seeping through the veins and arteries of England's cricketing body politic.

Austerity Bites

'Bradman did not get his hundred.'

Eric Hollies

THE immediate post-war years are remembered for the genius of Denis Compton. The Middlesex and England batsman scored 3,816 runs in the summer of 1947. Still only 29, despite making his England debut a decade earlier, he seemed to herald an entertaining future. It is often forgotten that Compton was a more than useful chinaman bowler who took 622 first-class wickets. He had everything!

Sadly English cricket in general was not so keen to provide excitement. The Second World War depleted the game more in England than Australia, hence the latter's easy Ashes wins in 1946/47 and 1948. As has been mentioned, the 1946 rule allowing a new ball every 55 overs was likely to hit leg-spinners and chinaman bowlers like Compton particularly hard. It cannot be a coincidence that, as the 1940s moved into the 1950s, the supply dried up.

'I am still under the impression that so potent was the drug of the new ball,' wrote Arthur Mailey, 'that some modern captains would have laid both Barnes and O'Reilly aside when the new "pill" was due to leave the umpire's pocket.'

The 1948 Ashes, in which Don Bradman's 'Invincibles' beat Norman Yardley's England 4-0, serves as an object lesson in how to mishandle leg spin. In the Headingley Test Australia scored 404 to win, then a record. Yardley's only genuine bowling options were a battery of medium pacers, rookie off-spinner Jim Laker and Compton's chinamen. As opener Arthur Morris and Bradman cruised to big hundreds, Yardley turned in desperation to Len Hutton to bowl his leg breaks. The Yorkshireman's four overs went for 30 runs, laying bare the lack of resources at England's disposal on a pitch which had deteriorated over several days of sunshine. It allowed the Australians to accelerate towards their total during the early stages of the run chase. Yardley was condemned for bowling Hutton. England's best chance to win a match in a horrendously one-sided series was lost.

Bradman knew why. 'I dislike being critical if it means being destructive, and I think little criticism is warranted here, but the one great error England made was in not having a leg-spinner like Wright or Hollies in the side,' he wrote. 'I still think we would not have made 250. No ball bowled is as difficult to handle as the one which leaves the bat and goes towards slips… It was in an effort to overcome this deficiency that Yardley used Hutton as a bowler, gave us most valuable runs and was roundly condemned for having done it.'

Yardley defended himself against 'severe criticism'. 'On a wearing wicket, we had no leg-spinners or slow left-armers with the exception of Denis Compton,' he argued. 'Hutton had bowled with good effect for Yorkshire on many occasions in such circumstances, and he might have got me a much-needed wicket.' Yardley added that he had wanted to tempt the Australians to score more quickly to increase the chance of wickets.

'Once again the situation demonstrated the folly of England taking the field in a home Test without a leg-spinner. How easy to be wise after an event. Yet the lesson of that day remains for future selections; a leg-spinner is essential, and his absence may in itself mean the loss of a game.'

Eric Hollies, by now in his mid-30s, was already a well-known figure in the game. In July 1948 he gave a talk on *BBC Children's Hour* entitled 'How I Learned Cricket'. Just to show not all change since this period has been for the worse, another item on the programme was 'The Coloured Coons: A Children's Darkie Minstrel Show'.

Not selected for England in the summer's Tests thus far, Hollies played for Warwickshire against the Australians in August, taking eight wickets in the first innings, including Bradman bowled. He noticed that some of the visitors' discomfort came from waiting to see the ball's movement off the pitch, rather than studying it through the air – and that Bradman was among the 'more confused'. He bowled Bradman a couple of googlies but held the delivery back after that. 'I had the definite impression he was not "seeing" the ball from my hand (perhaps not even looking for it), but was playing the ball late and hurriedly off the pitch,' he wrote.

Following England's humiliating failure to defend a 400-plus target at Headingley, Hollies was called up for the Oval Test. Initially he was reluctant to take part. He told Warwickshire secretary Leslie Deakins he would rather play for the county. 'The rubber had been settled, much of the interest seemed to have gone,' he recalled, adding, 'The only interest in the Oval Test seemed to centre around whether Bradman would get a century in his last Test match. However, the Warwickshire committee persuaded me to play – and Bradman did not get his hundred.'

Before the match Hollies discussed tactics with county captain Tom Dollery. He decided to base his approach on what had happened in the Warwickshire match, remembering that if called upon to bowl to him at the Oval he would 'bowl the googly to him second ball, just in case he was expecting it off the first delivery'.

The moment came. England were abject in their first innings at the Oval, being dismissed for 52. In fact, the 55-over rule played into Australia's hands throughout the season. Unlike the 1930s, when Clarrie Grimmett and Bill O'Reilly had been on the scene, Australia's strength was now in its pace attack of Ray Lindwall, Keith Miller, Bill Johnston and Ernie Toshack. The constant promise of a new ball kept the speedsters sharp. Leg-spinner Doug Ring was not even called upon to bowl during the

Oval carnage. English cricket had smacked itself *and* leg spin in general in the face.

Australia got to 117 by the time Hollies dismissed opener Sid Barnes, caught by wicketkeeper Godfrey Evans for 61. In came Bradman. Yardley and his men, sensing this was probably his last innings, unless the English batted far better second time around, raised their caps and gave three cheers. Hollies remembered Yardley turning to him beforehand and saying, 'We'll give him three cheers when he gets on to the square. But that's all we'll give him – then bowl him out.'

Bradman settled down, having taken his usual long walk to the crease to accustom his eyes to the light. The first ball Hollies bowled was a good-length leg break, which he defended.

It was now time to put the plan hatched with Dollery into action. The Don once again settled down and Hollies came in over the wicket. He turned his wrist around to bowl the googly. It landed just outside Bradman's off stump. Bradman, who moved three-quarters of the way to the ball's pitch, failed to smother it. The ball turned in and flew past his inside edge, or just tickled it, knocking into his middle and off stumps. He was out for a second-ball duck.

Surely this was not the way it was meant to end? Bradman's dismissal meant he concluded his Test career with an average of 99.94 runs. Had he scored just four runs it would have been 100. There is no such thing as perfection when it comes to a batting average as, theoretically, a player could never be dismissed, leaving it at infinity. But we count in multiples of ten, probably because that is how many digits we have, therefore giving extra lustre to the 100 figure. Hollies's success kept Bradman within the bounds of perceived humanity – just.

The googly, that cheeky ball Bernard Bosanquet had popularised almost half a century earlier, before the Australians had taken ownership, had come home.

'That reception had stirred my emotions very deeply and made me anxious – a dangerous state of mind for any batsman to be in,' Bradman recalled. 'I played the first ball from Hollies though not sure I really saw it. The second was a perfect length googly which deceived me. I just touched it with the inside edge of the bat and the bail was dislodged. So in the midst of my great jubilation at our team's success, I had a rather sad heart about my own farewell as I wended my way pavilion-wards.'

England were delighted. Wicketkeeper Evans saw Bradman off with the words, 'Hard luck, mate.' It was an ordinary man's language, spoken to a would-be god. It was appropriate, as Hollies's effort was one of ingenuity overcoming something other-worldly. Hollies was a man who made much of his own ordinariness. He did not enjoy the fuss over the Bradman dismissal but could regard it as a victory for the common man.

Hollies's single act came in a match in which England were once again thrashed. It was a rearguard gesture, both in terms of the match and the position of leg-spin bowling. The next decade saw its reduction to near insignificance.

Complex Times

'A ball turning in from a left-arm bowler
is not considered as dangerous as one
that turns away. The logic being that it
is not difficult to combat something that
moves towards you... It can be difficult
to combat something that moves towards
you, if it arrives unexpectedly.'

Chinaman, Shehan Karunatilaka

ERIC Hollies was ambivalent about the state of the art/craft he had given his working life to. In his 1955 autobiography he wrote that he could count those of his type 'on the fingers of one hand, and unhappily not a single leg-break bowler has established himself in county cricket since the war. But although the evidence may seem to be overwhelming, I think that leg-break bowling has faded temporarily rather than that it is in an advanced stage of dying out.'

Living until 1981, spending many years picking up wickets in the Birmingham League, he witnessed its near-total demise. His words of 1955 would prove to be horribly optimistic.

His contemporary Doug Wright played only one match, at Lord's, in the 1948 Ashes, but he continued to be a regular pick for England until 1951. He ended up with 108 wickets, his notorious bad luck with dropped catches and proneness to loose deliveries leaving him with an average of 39.11. Most famously, Bill Edrich dropped an easy catch at slip from Don Bradman off Wright's bowling in the fifth Test at Sydney in 1946/47, when Bradman was on just two. He went on to score 63 as Australia won by five wickets.

Another leggie who lost some of his best years to the war was Worcestershire's Roly Jenkins. Seldom can a cricketer have been so infatuated with his skill. He practised for hours in the nets before the start of play, constantly fretting about the 'mechanics' of his action. Jenkins, who made his first-class debut in 1938, was one of the eccentrics of the county circuit.

Usually bowling in his cap, in mid-flight he sometimes urged the ball, 'Spin for Roly.' He felt anthropomorphic kinship with the sometimes battered tool at his disposal.

Jenkins had to postpone his wedding when summoned to tour South Africa in 1948/49. He took a wicket with his third ball in Tests. Yet he never became established at international level, playing nine Tests.

There was no England place for Jenkins in the summer of 1949. At least he had time for the overdue honeymoon. Worcester released him for a week in June, and he sent the team a postcard from Llandudno saying, 'They say it's sunny outside.' Jenkins was more Australian than English, in that he turned the ball prodigiously. But he never played Tests there.

England picked three leg-spinners for the final game of the summer's series against New Zealand, as they desperately tried to prise out the visitors following three draws in a row in matches patronisingly scheduled for a maximum of three days each. Wright, Hollies and Freddie Brown were in the side, as was off-spinner Jim Laker. Even Compton bowled an over of his chinamen. Still the Kiwis held on to draw once more. Brown, leading the side, said he found it 'embarrassing' to have too many bowlers at his disposal. Hollies noticed the 'contrast to the previous year', when England had been reluctant to pick any leggies against Australia. After the famine came a belated and inedibly excessive feast.

In the late 1940s and 1950s English cricket started to do the once unthinkable. It bought in several experts from abroad. There was a growing belief that English leg-spinners and chinamen were irredeemably inferior to those from abroad. Australian chinaman bowler Jack Walsh, who realised his chances to make the Test team were limited, joined Leicestershire after the Second World War. He ended up with 1,190 wickets. Walsh's balls spun a great deal and, even if he lost his accuracy from time to time, they were always potent. George Tribe, another chinaman bowler who played three Tests for Australia against England in 1946/47, ending up with an average of 165, came to Lancashire league cricket. In 1951 he joined Northamptonshire, spending the rest of the 1950s as a county cricketer of considerable success. Another of their countrymen, flighty leg-spinner Colin McCool, gave fans at Somerset a 'manifestation of an art that was to disappear from English grounds', from 1956 to 1960, according to *Wisden*.

Nottinghamshire went one further, including two overseas leg-spinners in their side. One was Australian Bruce Dooland, who had played three Tests against England and India in the mid-to-late-1940s with little success. Still, famed particularly for his flipper, he was regarded as possibly the finest leggie in the world at the time, taking 748 wickets for his county in a five-year stay starting in 1953.

The other foreign star at Trent Bridge was Gamini Goonesena, a small, quick-paced leg-spinner from Ceylon who captained Cambridge University. Hollies remarked that the success of Dooland and Goonesena at Notts would do a 'great deal of good' to encourage youngsters to try leg spin.

Goonesena wrote a charming book of tips for youngsters, published in 1959. It was presented in the form of a cartoon dialogue between the reader and Goonesena himself. One reader's questions was, 'Is it possible for one player to help another actually on the field?'

'But of course,' Goonesena replied. 'When I was bowling for Notts in the days when Bruce was with us I might get slammed by a batsman for a couple of fours and a six in one over – and feel a little dispirited! Then, before my next over, he'd stroll over to me and say, "Let him take another four, Gami – but you'll get him with your next ball." And very briefly he'd proceed to tell me *how* I should get him. Nearly always it worked.'

It was a wonderful learning environment, the best of knowledge available to share at difficult times. Goonesena felt Dooland had been 'kind and helpful and it was thanks to his advice that I acquired confidence in my bowling and a much more acute knowledge of the tactic of the game than I'd had previously'.

What is striking is that two top players who never turned out for England, and were never likely to, were enjoying this relationship in county cricket. Goonesena's book was aimed at a universal audience, but where was the one-to-one help for English players? He moved to Australia soon afterwards, where he played for New South Wales for a couple of seasons.

Foreign leg-spinners and chinamen were taking over in county cricket. The process brings to mind gruesome events more than 300 years previously. In the early-to-mid-17th century many of the small states of what is now Germany went through the Thirty Years War, a complex combination of religious and dynastic disputes. It left a quarter of the population dead. In 1936 the Hungarian academic Baron de Wesselenyi wrote that the states involved had previously been a collective 'producer of culture', exporting art and music to other parts of the world. Following the bloodshed and political upheaval, their confidence destroyed, they became a 'receiver of culture', more content to be led than to innovate. This allowed the development of what Wesselenyi called a 'national inferiority complex'.

No sporting trauma can compare to what happened in central Europe in the first half of the 17th century. Yet a phenomenon of a broadly similar nature occurred in English cricket in the mid-20th century. The English no longer trusted themselves to create bowlers of the leg-spin type but perceived a magical ability in Australians to do so. Counties paid to receive and utilise the product of a healthier, more confident overseas culture. English cricket was buying in the leg break, googly and flipper expertise it had first created and was now forgetting. It got much worse as the years went on.

In the mid-1930s Eric Hollies bought a book, Clarrie Grimmett's *How to Bowl Leg Breaks*, en route to a match in Yorkshire. Sitting opposite him on the train was his captain for the match, Jack Parsons, a man of the Church who had won a Military Cross during the First World War. Parsons took the book from Hollies's hand and said, 'You don't want to bother reading how he bowls. Just carry on your own way.'

This was well and good for a player of that era, where leg-spin expertise was to be found throughout county cricket. By the 1950s the Dooland–Goonesena-type shared experience was becoming a rarity for Englishmen.

The 1950/51 Ashes tour starkly demonstrated the state of English leg spin. Doug Wright managed 11 wickets at just over 45 in the five Tests, but suffered from fibrositis. One dismissal of captain Lindsay Hassett with a fast leg break is regarded as one of the best deliveries in Ashes history, up there with Warne's ball. But it was a rare success on a difficult tour.

When asked about media reports ahead of the series that Don Bradman could make a return to the Australia side, England skipper Freddie Brown jokily referred to Eric Hollies, 'Well, it will be all right if he does. We've brought the man who got him out for a duck.'

The *Sydney Morning Herald* predicted good things. 'Hollies is a colt no longer,' it said. 'He has reached the stage when it is customary to look for less arduous relaxation, but he is still a remarkably good bowler who will be a tower of strength to the touring team, especially on our Sydney pitch.'

Just over two years after Hollies had bowled the googly that meant his name would live on throughout the cricketing world, he had a terrible tour of Australia, his first and only one. He called it 'one of the biggest disappointments' of his career. Hollies found that the ball would not turn in the nets, his finger spin not enough to make it deviate off the hard pitches. This was a relic of the 'rolling' style he had adopted in the early 1930s to ensure he could bowl with enough accuracy to cope with the type of onslaught he had experienced from Wally Hammond. It did not work in Australian conditions.

So Hollies slowed his pace, but then found that his main asset, containment, disappeared. County skipper Tom Dollery had once called Hollies 'the toothache bowler', such was his effect on scoring rates. Australia had rendered him toothless, even more than it had Tich Freeman. He never played for England again.

Even Brown, whom Aubrey Faulkner had converted from pace to leg spin two decades earlier, turned to gentle swing bowling instead at points, operating as a fill-in bowler. His mentor would not have approved.

Brown was disappointed with Hollies, who 'either bowled too quickly or too short – and when he tried to reduce his pace and to throw the ball up, the batsman seemed able to go down the wicket to him without danger. Being rather a roller of his leg breaks… he turned the ball very little indeed.'

Nor was Arthur Mailey impressed. At least he liked the company of the droll Hollies, the pleasant Wright and the fiery Brown. 'While England's slow bowlers on the whole might not possess the skill of those from Australia,' he said, 'they appear to be far more amusing and mentally stimulating.' In this series, Australian mystery spinner Jack Iverson took 21 wickets and off-spinner Ian Johnson took seven.

With the change in the LBW law already stacked against them, the 1950s saw another development to hinder leg-spinners. During the years 1946 to 1953, according to England batsman Colin Cowdrey, the game had been played on brown wickets on which bat dominated ball. These were not in themselves good for leg spin, as a lack of pace and bounce does not favour the style. But no one else had much of an advantage either.

The counties were worried about too many draws and an edict went out to groundsmen to prepare more 'sporting' conditions. This meant grassier pitches on which seam bowlers would prosper, the shine staying on the ball for longer. It had a similar effect to the previous allowance of a new ball every 55 overs a few years earlier (by now adjusted to 65 overs in county cricket), in that quicker bowlers had an ongoing advantage. It also coincided with an increase in the use of artificial fertilisers, making the outfield greener and less abrasive.

'If you now operate with a spinner at one end and a seamer at the other,' wrote Cowdrey in the mid-1970s, 'the seamer is liable to become volubly neurotic if he does not see the spinner polishing up the ball on his trousers or shirt between deliveries to keep it in "condition". Wilfred Rhodes or Doug Wright or Bill O'Reilly, indeed, most of the great spinners, would have resisted.'

On Sunday 26 April 1953, cricketers gathered at Stafford Cricket Club for a match to celebrate the 80th birthday of S.F. Barnes. The old man turned his arm over, as upright as ever, at an understandably lower pace. It was a reminder of better times.

The man becoming the most powerful in English cricket by this time, at least among the players, had taken against wrist spin. Possibly because of his humiliation in front of his home crowd at Headingley during the 1948 Ashes, Len Hutton was less than keen to use what might have been an effective weapon. As captain for the 1954/55 series, in which Frank Tyson and Brian Statham terrorised the Australians into submission, he was in an enviable position in terms of his pace attack.

Yet his county colleague Johnny Wardle, usually an orthodox left-arm spinner, offered something else. In the nets on board the ship taking the MCC side to the southern hemisphere he tried out his chinamen and googlies. A young Peter May was impressed, noting that he was 'high-class' and had a 'great gift of being able to bowl his chinamen and googlies without seeming to practise them'.

Hutton had seen it all long before, when he faced Wardle, then 24, in the nets at Yorkshire after returning from the 1946/47 Ashes tour. 'He bowled orthodox left-arm spinners to me for quite some time and without a word of warning produced a chinaman to be followed a few balls later by a googly,' said Hutton, 'both pitched on a perfect length. The chinaman turned considerably and the googly just enough to beat the bat. "That surprised you," called Johnny from down the net. Not only was I surprised, I was elated and my thoughts turned to the outstanding talents of this young cricketer.'

'I don't want to sound immodest,' recalled Wardle, 'but I have never seen a great player so much at sea.'

Despite this promise, Yorkshire ordered Wardle to focus on orthodox finger spin. It had been good enough for Bobby Peel, Wilfred Rhodes and Hedley Verity and would suffice now. The former England fast bowler Bill Bowes, now working as the county's bowling coach, reached a compromise:

> We had been trying to get Johnny into the Yorkshire orthodox tradition. But we soon realised that the best plan was to allow him to mix them. On turners he got the ball to bite with his orthodox slows. On good wickets he was able to achieve movement with his wrist spin. At that time it was amazing how few batsmen on the county circuit were able to 'tell' him.

So Wardle was told to hold back the wristy stuff for when nothing else was likely to work, something against which he bridled.

Wardle took 102 international wickets at 20.39 during his career. But he was hardly used for the first three Tests in which he played in 1954/55. It was only in the final match, at Sydney, where he got a proper run out with his chinamen, taking 8-130 in a draw. Ian Peebles declared that Wardle, spinning the ball a long way, had found his 'true metier on Australian pitches but it is doubtful if such eccentricities will be encouraged in Yorkshire where, in any case, his orthodox leg breaks (that is, ordinary slow left-arm deliveries) are probably more effective'.

Peebles's old friend Jim Swanton thought this performance made it 'clear what he might have achieved by this method if it did not go so much against the grain, in Yorkshire and England circles'. Even Bowes joined in, proclaiming, 'My word, what a tangle these Australians were in against the wristy spinners of

Wardle. I believe that Wardle, concentrating on this style of bowling, could keep his place in any side.'

Although England won the series 3-1, it might have been easier had Hutton unleashed Wardle earlier. A later England captain, Mike Brearley, bemoaned what he saw as a misuse of his talents. Orthodox slow left-arm could be an attacking force in England but chinamen would be more effective abroad, he argued. Hutton 'had a deep respect for fast bowling and an equally deep mistrust of leg spin', finding it 'disturbingly enigmatic', Brearley remarked. During one Middlesex versus Yorkshire match, Hutton was teased in the dressing room as his opponents came in for a chat. 'How is it that you Yorkshiremen have no idea against leg spin?' they asked.

'The further north you go, the slower they get,' replied Hutton, tapping the side of his head. In other words, he thought the softer pitches at Leeds, Bradford, Scarborough and the rest were not conducive and that leg-spinners, not to mention chinamen, were an expensive luxury. This climatic argument against leg spin and chinamen runs throughout modern English cricket. Pitches can be slow, it is argued. Fingers and wrists are less supple because of the damp and cold. But English weather is not permanently terrible. We would do well to remember that.

Hutton's successor as England captain, Surrey's Peter May, also erred on the side of caution when handling Wardle. In South Africa in 1956/57 the Yorkshireman took 26 Test wickets at 13.80. In the second Test, at Cape Town, May did not enforce the follow-on and England set the hosts 385 to win on a dusty, slow pitch. 'Peter realised that I was a match-winner on that particular wicket,' said Wardle. 'He spoilt it by asking me not to bowl the chinaman stuff at Trevor Goddard.'

Wardle replied that, on such a surface, bowling the orthodox stuff would be like giving the batsman net practice. Devilry was required. Wardle bowled chinamen at Goddard and soon got his man. He gave the ball air and allowed it to grip, taking 7-36 in the innings and 12-89 in the match. South Africa were all out for 72. 'The pitch did not break up much but he turned the ball huge amounts,' wrote May, 'and, apart from Roy McLean, no one had much idea of how to play him.'

Former England batting maestro Wally Hammond, who had tussled with Clarrie Grimmett and Bill O'Reilly in the 1930s, watched and proclaimed it was the best spin bowling he had seen. Someone asked how Wardle compared with Chuck Fleetwood-Smith, whose own chinamen and googlies had been so dangerous in the same era. 'He left the Australian standing,' Hammond replied. 'I have never seen anyone with such control as a wrist-spinner.'

May was cautious once more at Durban, as he looked to make the 2-0 lead in the five-match series unassailable. He again called on Wardle to bowl orthodox left-arm spin as South Africa were left with under 200 to chase. This time he agreed and the match ended in a draw, with South Africa six wickets down and 47 runs adrift.

'May ought not to feel that spin bowlers should be treated as delicately as Bristol glass,' Alan Ross wrote in *The Observer*. 'It is part of their scheme of things that the batsman should chance his arm against them, and they must be encouraged to keep the ball up, and to flirt with him, not discourage his attacking strokes as May required Wardle to do.'

There was also criticism of England's slow batting. England lost the next two Tests, to square the series at 2-2. Had May squandered the advantage?

The irony of the attitude passed down from Hutton to May was that Yorkshire could lay claim to having invented the chinaman. Batsman Maurice Leyland bowled it with success in the 1930s, at roughly the same time as Ellis 'Puss' Achong of the West Indies. Yet it remained so rare that only Wardle, Denis Compton and Leyland himself ever had much joy with it among Englishmen in the domestic game.

In 1950, R.L. Stewart wrote an article in *The Cricketer* explaining why it was so mistrusted. 'Not content with the leg break, the slow right-hander invented the googly. This was, perhaps, to be forgiven, for neither the leg break nor the googly is a natural ball. But there can be no forgiveness for the slow left-hander who tries to bowl the googly or "chinaman". Nature has given to the left-hander the most difficult ball of all, the ball which floats through the air and then turns back off the pitch and runs away towards first slip. To throw away this gift is quite unforgivable… here is a heresy which must be eradicated by every inquisitorial torture known to cricket coaches.'

A dislike of unorthodoxy confronted Yorkshire's own leg-spinner, the delightfully Anglo-Saxon-sounding Edric Leadbeater. He played for the side from 1949 to 1956 but Wardle and his right-arm colleague Bob Appleyard were preferred. Leadbeater, known as 'Eddie', had two Tests against India in 1951/52. Never awarded a Yorkshire cap, he played for two seasons for Warwickshire before retiring. 'At Yorkshire,' he said, 'when you ran in to bowl, always at the back of your mind you were thinking, "I hope this isn't a full toss… I hope this isn't a short one."'

Similarly, Johnny Lawrence was not wanted at Headingley after the Second World War and moved to Somerset, where he played with considerable success. He later returned to his native county, where he is best remembered as the mentor of Yorkshire and England opening batsman Geoffrey Boycott.

As the 1950s progressed England had the services of an outstanding group of finger spinners. Surrey's Jim Laker and Tony Lock dominated, but Wardle and Appleyard were not far behind. Laker's 19 wickets in the Old Trafford Test of 1956 showed the power of this type of bowling on a responsive pitch. Leg spin was being progressively overshadowed.

After Laker's famous performance, the writer Gordon Ross wondered in *The Cricketer* about the 'diminishing race' of leg-spinners. England and Essex all-rounder Trevor Bailey opined in 1955 that 'not one top-class post-war English leg-break bowler has come on the scene'.

There was a re-floating of the idea that the LBW law could alter so as to allow dismissals by balls pitching outside the leg stump. Laker was dismissive of such a 'nonsensical' idea, 'The game is cramped enough as it is, and it would be considerably worse with such a ruling. Although the present rule does handicap the genuine leg-spinner, I do not think such a change would encourage new leg-breakers as much as a race of pedestrian bowlers firing away from round the wicket and the extreme edge of the crease, in the hope of hitting the batsman's pad with angled deliveries, in exactly the same manner as the in-slant brigade do now.'

At the end of 1957 Doug Wright, Eric Hollies and Bruce Dooland retired. Between them they had taken more than 5,000 wickets. *Wisden* was pessimistic, saying the number of decent 'googly-type bowlers of any standing' left in English first-class cricket 'could afterwards be counted on the fingers of one hand'.

'The strategical and tactical changes in big cricket since the war have almost driven such bowlers out of the county game,' it added. 'In an age when field strategy is based on giving nothing away the googly bowler, who trades runs for wickets, has lost his popularity. County captains attend meetings at which they pay lip service to the need for encouraging attacking cricket. But, when they return to their counties, they discard venturesome batsmen and turn their backs on bowlers liable to give runs away, however great their wicket-taking potential may be.'

Yorkshire sacked Johnny Wardle in 1958 amid acrimony, depriving fans of even occasional glimpses of the chinaman/googly bowler. Roly Jenkins retired that year too.

All the while the game was becoming more professionalised, in a narrow sense. The distinction between gentlemen and players was not to disappear until the 1963 season, but within cricket freedom of expression was fading, under a more workmanlike, strangulatory form of captaincy alien to the old amateur ethos.

During the 1959/60 tour of the West Indies, England captain Peter May had at his disposal Lancashire's Tommy Greenhough, a leg-spinner who the previous summer had taken five wickets in an innings against India. Greenhough remains, to this day, the last Englishman to have achieved such a feat in a Test match. As *The Guardian*'s Mike Selvey has remarked, Harold Macmillan still had more than four years to serve as Prime Minister. Continuing the theme, pianist Russ Conway was at number one in the Hit Parade with 'Roulette'. The first hovercraft had been launched just a few days earlier. Wolverhampton Wanderers were English football champions. It was a long time ago. Fifty-six years and counting since the last England leg-spinner's 'five-fer'.

Greenhough badly injured his feet by falling 40 feet down a shaft while working in a cotton mill in 1950, aged 18, but he worked his way back to fitness. Sadly he missed the Test after his five-wicket haul, with problems he had running down the pitch enforcing some remedial work. He returned for the fifth Test of the summer and made it on to the 1959/60 West Indies trip.

Greenhough, who bowled above the normal spinner's pace, became the cause of one of several rows between captain May and vice-captain Cowdrey and the tour manager, that old England leggie Walter Robins. Robins had a big, abrasive personality. Cowdrey was not happy with his behaviour. He reported that, at dinner one night, he and May 'were still on the soup when Robins launched into a powerful peroration on how he expected Greenhough to be used on the tour. Peter May was nonplussed by his aggressive approach. He took a deep breath and all he could say was, "Waiter, may I have a little more toast, please?" and then proceeded to commend the excellence of the soup. Robins continued to harry us day after day, throughout the voyage, and with typical courtesy, but no lack of firmness, Peter May would not be drawn.'

Cowdrey complained of Robins's 'extraordinary histrionics' but neither May, nor Cowdrey, who led the side when May was injured, budged. 'It was the only time anyone could remember Colin Cowdrey getting passionate about anything,' Robins's son Richard says. May denied having any argument with Robins, but acknowledged that Greenhough 'was very much seen as a symbol of a new era'. Not for long.

While the supply of English leg-spinners was drying up, so was demand at the highest level. Robins, an old-school amateur entertainer, could not bear it. Cowdrey and May's strategy was anathema to him.

Greenhough returned to county cricket, finishing in 1966. By the end his action, always low-slung, had dipped to the extent that England off-spinner Ray Illingworth told him, 'I don't know if you realise, but you're bowling on your knees.' It serves well as an analogy for English leg spin by this time.

The 1950s were a decade of great loss. Richie Benaud, the Australian who kept world-class leg spin going into the early 1960s, found that, by the time the new decade began, there were only four men frequently bowling it in county cricket. Two of them, Ian Bedford and Walter Robins's son Charles, played for Middlesex, keeping that county's tradition going.

It was in 1960 that Greenhough's Lancashire team-mate Bob Barber made his Test debut against South Africa. Picked first as a big-turning leg-spinner who batted left-handed, coming in at number eight, he later developed into a high-class batting all-rounder. Colin Cowdrey was captain when he made his bow at Edgbaston. 'In my first Test I played as a bowler,' says Barber, 'and although I had tied the South African batsmen down and troubled them in a match at Lord's just before, I was expected to start to bowl with six fieldsmen on the edge, giving a run away for every push.'

Barber suggests that 'the attitudes and philosophies of captains, coaches and club chiefs' are crucial to the handling of leg spin. Some leaders, including Yorkshire and England's Brian Close, were always 'attacking, trying to get a bat out', while others wanted to 'prevent runs being scored, trying to get a batsman to play a rash shot in frustration'.

'Being asked to bowl after everybody else has decided the wicket is too dead and the batting side are well set at 200/2 is very different to being called to bowl by a captain who appears to believe in you and wants to get a batsman out before the ball is as large as a balloon,' adds Barber. 'Whilst being called upon to bowl the last over before lunch may be a shrewd move, it may also indicate the captain fears what might have happened if you had been asked to bowl earlier, especially on a cold day.'

Barber had problems with officialdom at Old Trafford and moved to Warwickshire, where his batting grew more carefree.

Bowling became more of a second string. 'In those days our teams did not communicate enough,' he says. 'Nobody ever asked me, "Do you fancy bowling on this pitch or against that bat?" I had little interest in being the "Aunt Sally" because others didn't want stick. I liked the role of being an attacking bowler who aimed to get a bat out as quickly as possible, but not of being a stock bowler. My technique was not suited to that. I spun a lot and made it bounce more than most.' He says he was converted to leg spin by the success of chinaman bowler George Tribe in the Lancashire leagues. Tribe, whose maxim, according to *Wisden,* was, 'Spin first, length afterwards,' was a friend of Barber's father and he followed his example, after an hour or two of coaching, in spinning the ball hard, in the Australian style.

Barber ended up with 42 Test wickets at an average of 43, placing him comfortably in the realm of useful international bowlers. In fact this total has only been beaten since the Second World War by Doug Wright among England leggies.

Barber argues that the culture of sport in general, not just cricket, changed during the 1950s and that 'the tendency was for negativity to increase'. There was more 'trying to win by stopping others doing something and you not making mistakes rather than trying to win by being more positive and doing something special and so dominating the opposition'.

It is sometimes stated that one-day cricket undermined spin, and leg spin in particular, because of its emphasis on containment. This would be to apportion blame anachronistically. As Benaud remarked, leg-spinners were 'on the way out well before limited-overs cricket', which did not get going in earnest until the Gillette Cup began in 1963.

'They went to cricket's scrapyard in the sky because of the murmur and rumour around the counties which had them classed as ineffective on pitches affected by rain,' he wrote many years later.

There appeared to be no way back to prominence. What was it like to be a young leg-spinner in such an environment?

Rage Against The Dying Of The Light

'Times had changed.'

Robin Hobbs

'At that age it's difficult to tell people to piss off and leave you alone.'

Warwick Tidy

A RECURRING theme among top leg-spin bowlers is the length and loneliness of the journey they must undergo. Bernard Bosanquet and Sydney Barnes developed their own styles over several years. Clarrie Grimmett had to emigrate from New Zealand to Australia and play for three different state sides before his talents gained international recognition. Tommy Greenhough went from being severely injured in a factory accident to the Test team over the course of a decade. Ian Peebles left Scotland and a safe career in banking to pursue his ambitions.

None faced a more dangerous journey than the 15-year-old Robin Hobbs. The aspiring leg-spinner used to leave his home in Dagenham, on the borders of Essex and north-east London, and cycle under the Thames through the traffic-filled Blackwall

Tunnel to a leisure centre in Lewisham, where Kent were holding nets for youngsters.

It was 1957 and Doug Wright was about to retire, so the county asked former wicketkeeper Les Ames – once Tich Freeman's accomplice – to search for a successor.

A few months before nets started, Hobbs, who had recently left Raine's Foundation School in Stepney, east London, and was working for the Employers' Liability insurance company in London, had been invited down to Canterbury to take part in trials.

'A hundred people turned up that day and I was picked as one of four to attend nets with Kent over the river at Lewisham Swimming Baths in the winter,' he says. 'Essex had shown no interest at that stage. But later, because I was an Essex boy, word got around and Essex told Kent they didn't want them approaching me and I signed with Essex. It was ridiculous because, at that stage, Essex were playing on green wickets and they had about 11 spinners on the staff anyway. It was hard work getting even to the second team.'

Hobbs ached for success. In a scene reminiscent of a young Don Bradman using a stick to hit a golf ball thrown against a water tank at home in Bowral, he spent hours as a boy repeatedly bowling a ball against the wall of an outbuilding behind his father's grocery shop.

'That's how I became a bowler,' he says. 'After that I used to take a dozen balls to Dagenham's Central Park and spend hours just bowling. It seemed to work. I reckon that, up until three or four years ago, if you'd put a blindfold on me, I could still pitch six balls within the size of a newspaper because I'd done it so often.'

Hobbs used to grab oranges and apples and spin them around in his right hand, exercising his wrist and fingers. He impressed one of his teachers, Basil Dowling, who ran the school first XI. 'It was just one of those things I could do. Even when I was seven or eight I bowled leg breaks. I could never bowl an off break. The action came naturally. I turned it a long way and pitched it in the right place and people didn't play it very well. I was fortunate.'

He kept practising. 'There's no shortcut,' Hobbs says. 'You've got to bowl, bowl, bowl, bowl, day in and out. And you've got to want to do it, whether it be a cold day or a fine day. But the kids haven't got the chance today because there are so many other things going on. They have computer games and TV to distract them.'

This sense of space to develop without too much pressure persisted at Essex, then one of the poorer-performing counties. Often, says Hobbs, in the days before a two-division County Championship, there was little to play for by mid-season. The lack of genuine competitiveness allowed more conversations between teams after play finished, usually in the bar. Hobbs spent time talking to Norman Gifford, a slow left-armer with Warwickshire, Worcestershire and England, the two of them sharing tips.

Hobbs made his county debut in 1961, aged 19. He played in 12 matches, taking 23 wickets at 28.65, statistics he can still reel off at will. Former England all-rounder Trevor Bailey was the captain. 'I think he took a shine to me,' says Hobbs. 'I was kind of lucky as he shielded me. Don't ask me why. I was in competition with a chap called Bill Greensmith at that time.'

Greensmith was a talented leg-spinner almost 12 years Hobbs's senior who took 77 wickets in 1962, a season in which Hobbs did not play, but the next year he lost form and Hobbs was back in. He took 32 wickets.

Hobbs, a genial character, was invited to join the International Cavaliers tour to Jamaica the following winter. The team, made up of old stagers like Denis Compton, Jim Laker and Godfrey Evans, had a roistering time abroad. According to Hobbs the wickets, unlike those in England, 'bounced like a table top'. He experimented with flight and dip and angles of spin, much like Bernard Bosanquet had done on an actual table top playing twisti-twosti in the late 19th century. Hobbs took 16 wickets in three first-class matches.

On the International Cavaliers tour another leg-spin bowler, Alan Castell of Hampshire, lost form and, according to Hobbs, 'did the right thing and took up seam bowling'. Hobbs enjoyed the extra bounce pitches offered. There is also a sense that Hobbs, under the loveably reprobate guidance of Compton, Evans et al entered manhood during that winter. 'That actually made me,' says Hobbs. 'I was a different person.'

The 1964 season saw a county breakthrough, Hobbs taking 81 wickets at 28.91. That winter he was picked to go to South Africa with England under MJK Smith. There was some excitement in the press. 'I had one or two people like Keith Miller or the recently retired Richie Benaud, who'd written articles about me being the next great leg-spinner,' he says. 'It was rubbish, of course, but they really trumpeted my cause.' Hobbs did not play in the Tests.

He took 75 wickets in 1965 and 88 in 1966, his average also improving. In 1967 he made his Test debut at Headingley. England were playing India, no slouches against spin. Captain Brian Close assured him he would play the whole series.

The Headingley Test is most remembered as the one after which Geoffrey Boycott was dropped for batting too slowly in making 246 not out. Hobbs had a decent match, getting 3-45 in the first innings and 1-100 in the second. He indeed saw out the series, staying in the side for the first Test against Pakistan that summer. He was unlucky at Lord's against Pakistan, having Hanif Mohammad dropped several times on his way to 187 not out. Hobbs took 1-46, but reckons he could have had five wickets with a little bit of fortune, which 'could've changed my life'.

Outside cricket, the 'summer of love' was going on. When Hobbs made his debut in June, 'Silence is Golden' by the Tremeloes was at number one. This was succeeded by the more hippyish 'Whiter Shade of Pale' by Procul Harem, The Beatles' 'All You Need is Love' and 'San Francisco (Be Sure to Wear some Flowers in your Hair)' by Scott MacKenzie. All around was flower power and peace. The frilly-collared male aesthetic – mocked in recent years by the Austin Powers films – had a decidedly Edwardian tinge. Surely leg spin, with its atavistic, non-physical, even mind-bending associations would have been ripe for a comeback. Leg spin in the sky with diamonds? Unfortunately cricket, unlike youth culture, was more imbued with the spirit of those who had served in the war or done National Service, only abolished in 1960.

'There were certain people like John Woodcock, of *The Times*, who were very pro-leg spin in their reporting,' says Hobbs. When the selectors announced Hobbs was in his first Test squad, Woodcock wrote that he would be the first specialist England leg-spinner since Tommy Greenhough in 1960, all-rounder Bob Barber and Ken Barrington, primarily a batsman, having put in the overs. 'Leg-spin bowling, unlike bowling at medium pace, calls for more craft and touch than industry,' according to Woodcock's report. 'It is associated with sunshine and freedom of expression and many of the best things in cricket. For having been chosen, Hobbs may pass a word of thanks to Brian Taylor, his new county captain, who has given him every opportunity, even in the persistent floods rather than the darling buds of May.'

Taylor had indeed encouraged Hobbs to bowl with flight and turn. But tossing the ball up against the Indians seemed a little cavalier to the thoughtful newcomer. 'Hobbs… was not out of his element,' wrote Woodcock in *The Cricketer*, 'although he will find few better players of leg spin than these Indians, who feed on it at home. It is only a pity that he doesn't trust himself to give the ball a little more air a little more often.'

After that summer Hobbs played only three more Tests, against West Indies and Pakistan, finishing in 1971. Bishan Bedi, a beautifully poised Indian left-arm spinner but not much of a batsman, accounted for five of his 12 wickets at 40.08. They are decent figures in the context of so many matches against sub-continental sides.

'Times had changed by then,' Hobbs says. 'Derek Underwood had arrived. Norman Gifford was on the scene and [off-spinner] Pat Pocock to some extent.'

Hobbs, who lives in the Essex countryside, is unexpectedly lacking in self-assurance for someone who reached the highest level. 'I don't know whether I was quite good enough to play Test cricket,' he wonders. 'I have my doubts in some respects, but I'm not alone. There's a few who played Test cricket.'

Older observers at around the time of Hobbs's Test career were divided on what the future held for leg spin. Denis Compton saw 'brighter times ahead' with the likes of the Essex player on the scene. He was 'able to clown in the field without detracting from his ability. Such personalities should be encouraged. If more players were allowed to express themselves naturally, our legislators would find half their problems on the way to being solved. Cricket is too splendid a game to be muted by dull attitudes.'

Father Marriott was less optimistic. Shortly before his death in 1966 he took umbrage at a television commentator who remarked that, during Yorkshire's most successful era, the 1930s, championships had been won without a leg-spinner. Marriott bemoaned a 'widespread prejudice' in the media that this style of bowling had to be inaccurate. It was 'taken for granted that a leg-spinner is a heavy gamble because he cannot control the ball with real accuracy'. Marriott for one had belied this prejudice, as did Hobbs.

There is a suggestion that Trevor Bailey, a superb defensive batsman who had saved England on many occasions, used Hobbs too much in a containing role in his early days at Essex. Mike Brearley, after his time as Middlesex and England captain, wrote,

> Hobbs always claimed that his captain wanted him to bowl like a slow left-armer. The result was that Hobbs lost his ability to spin the ball sharply and became exactly what his captain wanted; he even drifted the ball in, like the left-armer. But this may, in fact, have been his best chance of building a career, and surviving in a form of county cricket which already included one-day matches. Possibly, too, Essex were never in his formative years powerful enough as a side to be able to afford a potential match-winner who was also quixotic and experimental.

Hobbs was certainly tight. His economy rate for England was 2.23. He regards Brearley's analysis as 'spot-on'. During his early days, Essex had a seam-heavy attack which decided Bailey's tactics. Bailey had been a pupil of Father Marriott at Dulwich College. Perhaps Marriott's perception of leg spin at its best being quick and relatively flightless had influenced him.

Bailey wrote that he had been 'weaned' on leg spin and had tried it himself as a boy, 'much to the joy' of Marriott. 'My action was graceful, almost poetic,' he recalled, 'but there was a minor weakness, my inability to turn the ball because my fingers were too small, but I would dearly have loved to have been able to bowl them well.' Bailey subscribed to Marriott's ideas, agreeing that the googly was 'less important than the top spinner', with its lower risk and more subtle deception.

Hobbs's first-class career was a very good one. He became the last English leg-spinner to take more than 1,000 wickets, ending up with 1,099 at 27.09.

'I didn't spin the ball very much in first-class cricket,' he says. 'I was fairly accurate. As the years went on there were four main leg-spinners in the county game: Intikhab Alam for Surrey, Mushtaq Mohammad, Harry Latchman and myself. So there were four people there who probably bowled upwards of 500 or 600 overs a year. But nowadays the game's changed. Unless you are very, very good – I mean exceptionally good – as a spin bowler, you've got to have something else, to be a batsman or a bloody fine fielder.'

Harry Latchman, who turned out for Middlesex and Nottinghamshire from 1965 to 1976, was a stocky, flighty, Jamaican-born bowler, who took almost 500 first-class wickets. He was a popular player who later coached at Merchant Taylors' School. The writer Rob Steen watched him as a boy. 'For those entranced by tales of Sonny Ramadhin but too young to have seen his artistry in the flesh, here was a suitably roly-polyish substitute,' he remembered. 'To a nine-year-old, leg spin seemed the most exotic form of athletic alchemy, and in the Summer of Love it was almost as rare as a head unadorned by flowers.'

As the 1960s moved into the 1970s, glam rock replacing flower power at the top of the charts, Edward Heath's Conservatives taking over 10 Downing Street from Harold Wilson's Labour, another young man was picked out as a future star.

The name Warwick Tidy is splendidly old-fashioned. It brings to mind Warwick Armstrong, the huge leg-spinning captain of the 1921 Australian touring team. It also evokes the name of the side Birmingham-born Tidy played for: Warwickshire. Neither was the reason for his mother's choice of name. She was a fan of the novelist Warwick Deeping, whose best-selling works in the 1920s and 1930s attempted to evoke the simpler delights of the Edwardian era. Given Tidy's career choice, this tribute to a creator of nostalgia was entirely apposite.

He made his debut for Warwickshire in 1970, aged just 17, when the Edgbaston pitch was at its flattest and the team needed something, anything, different to help take wickets on it. Warwickshire were a team of stars, including England batsmen M.J.K. Smith and Dennis Amiss and the West Indian pair of off-spinner Lance Gibbs and batsman Rohan Kanhai.

'Funnily enough I really didn't find it intimidating at all,' says Tidy. 'It may sound bloody stupid, but I just turned up, ran in and bowled. There were some people there who were very good to me, who took me under their wing. Nobody took the piss or made my life difficult, even though I was playing with some of the greatest players of the time.

'M.J.K. Smith was the best captain I've ever played under. He was so relaxed he calmed you down. He would come up to you two overs before a spell and say, "All right, Warwick, fancy a roll?" It was funny and it set me at ease. M.J.K. was a subtle captain.' The 1970 season was a good one for Tidy. He took 48 wickets for the first team at 31.12.

Growing up on a farm near The Belfry golf course, he and his brother spent most of their free time playing sport. Wrist spin came early and easily. 'I think I was about eight or nine,' says Tidy. 'I just started to bowl out of the back of my hand. But when I started all I bowled was googlies. I passed my 11-plus and went to grammar school. The sports teacher asked if I could bowl a leg break too and I answered that of course I did. He told me that bowling googlies all the time was no use and that I should focus on leg breaks, with the googly as a variety ball. That was good advice.'

Tidy's talent was noticeable and he played for two years for Warwickshire's under-15s. He had little coaching, relying on his ebullience and natural ability. Tidy left school after his O Levels and signed forms with Warwickshire. Following his excellent first year, the situation at Edgbaston became more difficult, as serious doubts entered his mind for the first time.

He started receiving advice, most of it not as good as that passed on by his sports teacher at school. 'It was well meant. Stuff like "speed up" or "slow down". When you are 17 or 18 you are very impressionable. You only think many years later, "Why did I listen to that?"

'At that age it's difficult to tell people to piss off and leave you alone. I never tell people what to do in that way when I'm coaching. You've got to work with what you've got and nurture it gently and softly. If it's not bust, why fix it?'

In 1971 Tidy took 23 wickets at 40.69. His success in 1970 had been based on pushing the ball through at a skiddy pace, using revolutions on the ball to achieve dip through the air, rather than tossing it up. Like Walter Robins in the 1930s, when told to slow down, he became confused about his best method. Warwickshire won the County Championship in 1972, but Tidy played in just one match. His only appearances in 1973 and 1974 were against Oxford and Cambridge universities. At the end of 1974 he was sacked, aged 22.

Tidy did not try to join another county, earning more in his other jobs than he had on the Warwickshire staff. There was talk of a move to Hampshire after he played a couple of matches on a social tour to Alderney, home of the cricket writer John Arlott, who came from Basingstoke and recommended a look at him. It never happened.

'I was speaking to Richie Benaud in the nets one day,' says Tidy. 'He said the best wrist-spinners didn't mature until later.' Warwickshire were not so patient.

Tidy worked as a rep for the medical technology firm Smith & Nephew then started at a building society, eventually becoming manager. He moved to Devon, working for several years as a financial adviser, and now runs his own gardening business, where his friendly, outgoing nature is valued.

After his sacking by Warwickshire, Tidy told a local newspaper he would do 'exactly the same thing again and bowl in the same way, but I'd block off my ears to some of the advice I was given'.

'The advice was meant in good faith,' he says with more than 40 years of hindsight. 'It wasn't meant to screw me up, but you have to be very careful with leg-spinners. Even now it really hacks me off that there's a lot of negative talk about wrist-spinners. People say they are very inaccurate. I say, "Think of Shane Warne." A wrist-spinner is going to take wickets. It just gets to me at times when people say it's a bit of a luxury.'

By the time Tidy played, first-class pitches were being covered outside the hours of play. This precluded the sticky wickets which had once benefited off-spinners. Leg spin offered a way to coax some life out of even the deadest pitches, but most counties hardly considered the idea. The gradually acquired habit of containment at the expense of adventure had become ingrained.

'Before the end of uncovered wet wickets we had a growth of what I used to describe as "phantom seamers" – medium-paced bowling, short of a wicket-taking length, whose aim was to cut down scoring rates,' says Bob Barber. 'They hoped that the seam of the ball on hitting the wicket would cause the ball to deviate in some way unknown to the batsman or themselves and so put doubt in a batsman's mind. Batsmen wanted to be on the retained list in August so they took few risks.

'I'm not convinced that covered wickets brought oppor-tunities for wrist spin, although they might have if leadership on and off the field had been positive and if sport had, as part of the entertainment business, concerned itself more with entertaining and not just winning.'

Australian Kerry O'Keeffe played for Somerset in 1971 and 1972, taking 96 wickets. Hobbs retired in 1975, a year after Tidy, but Glamorgan tempted him back in to the game in 1979, before he finally hung up his boots in 1981.

'Hobbs would have been a typical county spinner if he had been born 60 years earlier,' wrote Christopher Martin-Jenkins. 'As it happened he was for much of his career unique.'

Hobbs continued to turn out for club sides and Old England for many years. 'I started bowling leg spin at seven and played up until 68 years old,' he says. 'I look back on my career and I'm very content.' Will any future English leg-spinner get the chance to emulate his achievements?

Nadir, Qadir
And Clarke

*'I'd played a three-day game without
anyone knowing my name.'*

Andy Clarke

'**M**OST commentators go all gooey and sentimental
when a leg spinner comes on to bowl,' wrote Rob
Eastaway in *What is a Googly?*, an explainer of
cricket's terminology, 'because for many years seeing a leg-
spinner was as rare as spotting a black rhino.'

It is not a bad parallel. The global wild black rhino population
saw a 96% decline between 1970 and 1993, from 65,000 to 2,300.
Thanks to a well-organised conservation effort this has since
risen to about 5,000.

Leg-spinners, like rhinos, had a tough time of it in the 1980s.
Slow bowling in England itself became even more associated
with containment. Televised Sunday League matches showed
spinners, usually off-spinners, spearing the ball into middle-and-
leg stumps. Flight disappeared. Even top-quality spinners like
Middlesex and England's John Emburey lost the ability to take
first-class wickets for periods, such was their emphasis on keeping
the run-rate down on a Sunday or whenever a knockout one-day
competition was going on.

Yet this format of cricket cannot be blamed for the demise of leg spin in England, because Test captains were shunning it as early as the 1950s. One-day cricket, taking off in the 1960s, merely emphasised and reinforced a negative culture in bowling which had been developing for years. One would need a rhino's hide to dare to bowl tossed-up leg spin in such a climate.

The rise of West Indies to become the undisputed best team in the world, usually relying on a four-man pace attack, made slow bowling in general look quaint. Leg spin in particular.

David Lemmon, biographer of Tich Freeman, calculated that in 1980 in English county cricket only ten men had bowled any leg breaks. Most of these were batsmen who occasionally had a twirl. Two of the others were Robin Hobbs and Pakistani Intikhab Alam. A year later even they were gone.

After Hobbs there were no frontline English leg-spinners left. No one to pass on the skills honed by Allan Steel, Bernard Bosanquet, Sydney Barnes, Tich Freeman and all the others.

More pitches favoured seam bowling, such as those Richard Hadlee and Clive Rice operated on to such effect for the successful Nottinghamshire side of the early 1980s. Further advances in fertilisers meant ever more verdant outfields and that the ball kept its shine for even longer than had been the case in the 1950s and 1960s.

Derbyshire's Kim Barnett, best known as an England batsman, started his career as a promising leg-spinner. But he never got going, his best return being seven wickets in the 1980 season. He switched to occasional seam bowling.

The only glimpses most English fans got of leg spin were when foreign teams brought their own. Australia gave 38-year-old Bob Holland a debut in 1984. He played four matches in the 1985 Ashes series won by David Gower's England, taking just six wickets at almost 80, but keeping the runs down. Queenslander Trevor Hohns was 34 when he made his bow in 1988. He did well in England in 1989, taking 11 wickets at 27.27 as Australia recaptured the Ashes.

Bill O'Reilly, who had a few years left in him, was still reeling in 1985 about the change in 1946 which had allowed a new ball every 55 overs. Even though it had been hugely amended, he reasoned that the lusher outfields meant even a less generous allowance for fast bowlers militated against leg spin. 'Why even now, when the cricket world is crying out for spin bowling, is the new ball allowed after 85 six-ball overs?' he asked.

Throughout this decade of the Big Bang in the City of London and big hair on TV shows such as *Dynasty* and *Dallas* there was one man who really set hearts aflutter. His name was Abdul Qadir. I have to admit a certain bias here. Qadir is my favourite cricketer. Making his Test debut as a 22-year-old in 1977 he swerved, spun and schemed his way to prominence as part of the brilliant Pakistan team marshalled by Imran Khan. Qadir bounded up to the wicket, his arms became a flurry and there, suddenly, appeared the most beautiful variety of balls, spinning this way and that. It was all so aesthetically pleasing.

His leg break turned sharply. His top spinner bit and bounced. His googlies (for he was said to have at least two varieties) surprised batsmen, especially those brought up in England. His flipper skidded.

If the early 20th century cliché had been to call leg-spin/ googly bowlers 'merchants', who liked to deceive, Qadir was the living proof that clichés only became clichés because they contain some truth. He admitted his whole approach was based on mis-selling. His energetic run-up and action were designed to bombard the senses before the ball had been released. He even, at the suggestion of Imran, grew a goatee beard prior to the 1982 tour of England to enhance his mystical image.

India's batsmen, used to such a bowling style, were not fooled by Qadir. England's were. Unlike other Pakistani greats of his era, such as Imran, Javed Miandad and Wasim Akram, Qadir never played in county cricket. He maintained a distance from the English game.

He ended up with 82 wickets against England at just under 25 apiece. That is only slightly worse than Shane Warne's average.

His overall average in Tests was more than 32. Qadir's best year against England was 1987, when he took 7-96 in the first innings of the final Test at the Oval. 'The diet of fast bowling (much of it short) and seam on which batsmen the world over now exist,' wrote John Woodcock in *The Times*, 'is no preparation for making light of Qadir's wrist spin.' He took 13-101 in the first match of the return series in Lahore a few months later. This included 9-56 in the first innings.

Shane Warne wrote that cricket owed 'a great debt' to Qadir for keeping leg spin going. 'I like to think I have played a part in making it fashionable again, but I hope people don't forget the part played by Qadir in the history of cricket.'

Qadir was the culmination, in English cricket's imagination, of the idea that leg spin was exotic and foreign. He was part of a succession of effective Indian and Pakistani leg-spinners. Bhagwat Chandrasekhar of India, one arm withered by childhood polio, bowled an assortment of brisk leg breaks and top spinners. He took 16 wickets in three Tests against England in 1967, the series in which Robin Hobbs made his debut. He helped India win their first Test in England in 1971.

Chandrasekhar followed Vinoo Mankad in the 1940s and 1950s and Subhashchandra Pandharinath Gupte, known as 'Fergie', who worked his wiles in the early 1950s. Intikhab Alam and Mushtaq Mohammad bowled leg breaks for Pakistan to good effect in the 1960s and 1970s. Both appeared in county cricket, playing for Surrey and Northamptonshire respectively.

In January 1988 a little moustachioed, bespectacled leg-spinner, Narendra Hirwani, took the sensational figures of 16-136 in his Test debut at Madras, on a pitch of dubious quality. This beat the record of 16-137 taken by Australian swing bowler Bob Massie in his first Test at Lord's in 1972. Hirwani's feat came just a few weeks after Qadir's great successes against England. Leg spin was not a lost cause. If only someone in England would take it up.

Finally, after years of fatalism, there came a response. English cricket's answer to Qadir, Hirwani, Chandrasekhar and the rest was not a figure wrapped in hackneyed ideas of eastern exoticism. He was an insurance underwriter from Brighton.

Andy Clarke had been knocking around the Sussex league scene for several years by the time the county seriously started taking notice of him during the mid-to-late-1980s. In fact it shaped his whole outlook and style.

Clarke, born in 1961, began as a fast bowler but turned to leg spin when a coach noticed him trying it while warming up for an under-14s festival and suggested he took it up. A teacher had told Clarrie Grimmett the same thing at the start of his long apprenticeship in New Zealand about 70 years earlier. 'I took a wicket with my first ball,' says Clarke. 'We won the trophy and I never bowled anything other than leg spin after that.'

Clarke played for Brighton Schools and Sussex under-15s. No more representative honours came for another six years. In 1978 he entered the Spin for England competition, one of the occasional initiatives when the first-class game looks around for talent in form of an open contest. Clarke, the only leg-spinner on view that day at Old Trafford, made it to the last six, but was disheartened to be the one boy not approached by a county afterwards. Some of the comments about his style irked him. 'Too expensive' said one observer. 'Need a googly' said another. 'Need to be a top-order batsman' added a third.

Clarke played once for the Sussex second XI, aged 19, in 1981, but batted number 11 and did not bowl. 'When the travel expenses were handed out after the game,' he says, 'I can remember my envelope had a question mark instead of my name. So I'd played a three-day game without anyone knowing my name.'

Clarke started doing well for Preston Nomads in the Sussex League. Survival for a leg-spinner in the early 1980s involved adapting. 'I had to teach myself to bowl in a way that would allow me to bowl a lot of overs in a cricket league overrun with medium pacers,' he says. 'It was obvious from very early on that the "one or two bad balls an over" were going to limit my contribution to a league full of good-quality club players and ex-pros. So I started practising bowling more variations but with less genuine side

Allan Gibson Steel was a hugely successful leg-spinner, but he saw limited potential for its development. Roger Mann

Joe Vine bowled quick leg breaks, perhaps in an effort to overcome his batting frustrations. Sussex CCC Museum

Bernard Bosanquet popularised the googly, raising the expectations placed on leg-spinners. Roger Mann. *But Bosanquet faced ridicule when he first unveiled his new delivery in the nets at Oxford University.* Times Media

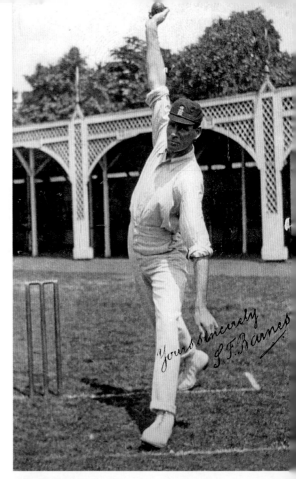

SF Barnes developed a stiff-wristed, fast leg break which has never been equalled. Roger Mann

South Africa's Aubrey Faulkner (batting) became obsessed with replicating the genius of SF Barnes. Patrick Ferriday

Alf 'Tich' Freeman broke wicket-taking records but failed to attract much attention from the England selectors. Roger Mann

Australia's Arthur Mailey (far left) was criticised for giving advice to England's Ian Peebles.

Charles 'Father' Marriott had a sensational Test debut in 1933 – his only match for England. Roger Mann

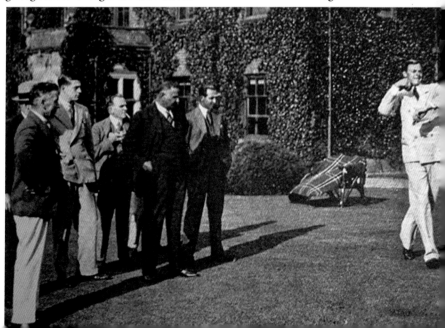

Walter Robins played for many years, but his effectiveness declined after being advised to slow down. Getty

Doug Wright had an eccentric run-up, but remains England's most successful Test leg-spinner. Roger Mann

A well-planned googly from Eric Hollies kept Don Bradman's Test average below 100. Getty

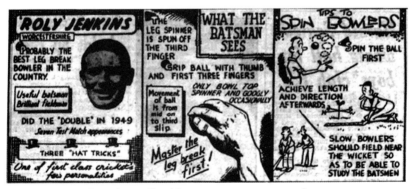

The eccentric Roly Jenkins offered his tips to newspaper readers.

After Bob Barber, no specialist leg-spinner played for England in the Ashes for 35 years. Roger Mann

Robin Hobbs was the last English leg-spinner to take 1,000 first-class wickets. Getty

Warwick Tidy made his first-class debut at 17 and was sacked at 22. Warwick Tidy Collection

Sussex's Andy Clarke struggled for many years for recognition that his leg spin could be effective in first-class cricket. Preston Nomads CC

Ian Salisbury had a good county career, but never secured a permanent England place. Sussex CCC Museum

Chris Schofield made a remarkable comeback for England after his county side sacked him. Getty

Scott Borthwick played one game for England in the 2013/14 Ashes – dismissing Brad Haddin and three others. Getty

The future: Can Adil Rashid become a fixture at international level? Getty

spin on the ball, therefore becoming more accurate and more of a viable option to the club captain. It was not long before I went from bowling four or five overs in situations where the game was already won or lost, to bowling the sixth over on a Saturday and bowling all the way through.'

Clarke says he requested a proper trial with Sussex, but received no reply. MCC said he was too old to join the Lord's ground staff. So Clarke continued in league cricket. 'I was one of the leading wicket-takers and it was demoralising to see so many spinners from outside the county being given trials. Even if I was not good enough, I wanted to be given the opportunity to see for myself and would not give up hope until I was given that chance.'

In 1987 Jim Parks, the former England and Sussex wicketkeeper-batsman, by then the club's temporary second XI coach, recommended another look at Clarke. He played a few matches and took wickets. Clarke says this 'embarrassed' Sussex into offering him a contract.

At the same time, Qadir was reaching his peak on the international scene. 'Abdul Qadir certainly influenced my decision to change to bowling leg breaks in the early stages of my cricketing life,' says Clarke. 'I don't think he influenced Sussex at all. I think it was just the number of wickets I was taking consistently in the Sussex League.'

In 1988 Clarke made his County Championship debut. Instantly observers started calling him a 'roller', a criticism of the lack of turn he had actually cultivated to ensure he could hold his place in league cricket. 'What I had learned to do was bowl in a way that is now recognised as a form of bowling that most countries, counties, or IPL or Big Bash teams have in their squads to open or bowl at the "death",' says Clarke. 'I was constantly told I needed to spin the ball more and needed a genuine googly to be successful, that I wouldn't get good players out unless I had the "normal" leg-spinner's variations. The fact that there are so many successful spin bowlers these days that use the crease and bowl top spinners or sliders as a variation proves beyond doubt that spinners play a bigger role these days without the need for a "miracle ball" Warne or Murali could bowl.'

Clarke had a promising first season for Sussex, taking 44 first-class wickets at 37.50. Unsurprisingly, given he had developed his style for league cricket, he took 17 one-day wickets at 15.70. Yet his time at Sussex was not to be a happy one. 'I think being 26 years old and straight out of club cricket meant I never really had the grounding and the discipline that I would have had if I'd been a 17-year-old and learning the ropes in the "normal" way,' he says. 'So here I was going straight in to the first team, without completing the apprenticeship and hard yards the senior players had gone through.' Some colleagues resented what they ironically thought had been an easy journey, he claims.

The team was struggling. 'I didn't have anyone to advise or help me because I didn't fit in with the cliques of three or four players in the dressing room,' Clarke adds. 'There were several occasions where I'd sit in the opposition dressing room at the end of a day's play just to avoid the situations – bullying some would call it – in an unhappy Sussex dressing room.'

Clarke says he was humiliated on several occasions. Once he was informed he was not in the starting XI only after he had walked through the Long Room on to the turf at Lord's. He was told to lose weight and was ignored in the dressing room after dropping a catch, the kind of treatment Kevin Pietersen has complained of by England bowlers in his recent autobiography.

Clarke's second first-class season, 1989, was a strange one. The bowling opportunities dried up, but his nine wickets cost only 24.66 each. He was feeling seriously undervalued, having given up his job in insurance to play. He was paid £7 a day, compared with the £40 his normal work provided.

'I have a wife and a mortgage but I played last season for peanuts because I was so thrilled at getting the chance to do something I had always dreamed of doing,' Clarke said in an interview in *The Cricketer*. 'I thought I had done enough to be treated better by Sussex. By offering me such a low wage – the bare TCCB [Test and County Cricket Board] minimum – they are looking on me as they would a 19-year-old.' Sussex said the salary structure, based on seniority and experience, was strictly controlled and they could not make allowances for individual players.

The future England bowler Ian Salisbury, a more classical leg-spinner with his wristy delivery and googly as variation, was by now on the Sussex books. He and Clarke spent a day being coached by Richie Benaud. 'He said about three words to me all day and that was about the dinner,' says Clarke. 'Because Ian Salisbury was an orthodox leggie he spent more time with him than me. I'm not saying he wasn't right in thinking Salisbury was better. I was as different to him as an off-spinner would be, and it was just a mistake to compare us.'

Clarke likens his style to that of India's Anil Kumble, who once admitted he did not turn the ball away from the right-hander but managed to take 619 Test wickets with his quick-through-the-air variations. 'Because I didn't spin the ball sideways as much as others I needed to be more accurate and I used to bowl top spinners a lot, particularly in one-day cricket – a slow top spinner which sometimes bounced a bit. Another variation was a slider, which was my most effective delivery and if the direct referral system they use now for LBWs on TV had been available, I'd have been more successful. I think that it was a mistake trying to change me into a conventional leggie.'

Sussex, who had picked Clarke for his success in league cricket, found his unusualness, not just as a leg-spinner but as a non-conventional leg-spinner, too much. He played the second half of the 1989 season and all of 1990 in the second XI. In his final second XI match he took 7-39. But at the end of the 1990 season Sussex decided instead to go with Salisbury. 'I remember being sacked by Norman Gifford, who was the coach at Sussex at the time,' he recalls. 'He said, "Clarky, you couldn't f***ing turn it on a corrugated roof," and "Good batters won't get out to you." At that point I turned and walked out of his office.'

Clarke coached in South Africa and, after recovering from a serious car accident in 1991, played for Buckinghamshire while working as a teacher. He played some second XI matches for Derbyshire in a vain attempt to return to the first-class scene. After that he turned out for Norfolk and Buckinghamshire again, playing on until 2009, when he was 47. He took almost 3,500 wickets in total for all sides.

His Sussex career was short and bittersweet. 'My best memory was bowling a maiden to Viv Richards in a one-day game,' says Clarke, who now lives in Scotland. 'He was the best on the planet and a hero of mine.' Most English leg-spinners of the 1980s would not have asked for more than that.

Salisbury

*'I think I was treated particularly
harshly. That stuff scars you but you
have to cope with it.'*

Ian Salisbury

I AN Salisbury was not a lucky bowler. He had two great
misfortunes in life. One was to be a leg-spinner in England.
The other was to play at the same time as Shane Warne.

'Warnie has made leg spin fashionable and took it to a higher
level,' he once said. 'I know I can never be as good as him. He is
just the best there's been.'

We have all seen what Warne has done. The most elusive
skill in cricket *can* be mastered. Such, though, is the reverence
in which this recently departed superstar is held that, while
he popularised leg spin as a spectacle, he arguably impeded its
development among others. We watched in wonder. Some did
more than watch, though. Some sought to emulate. For several
years Ian Salisbury had that task.

The name Shane Warne, just two monosyllables, rolls – or
rather leaps – off the tongue. It has an onomatopoeic quality.
One could say that Warne's best deliveries 'Shaned' (swerved) in
towards a batsman's pads, then 'Warned' (spun) away sharply to
take out the off stump or catch the edge of the bat.

If fast bowling has a sense of bravado, so did Warne's leg
spin. The more miles per hour the likes of Michael Holding and

Jeff Thomson got on the ball the more feared they became. The incredible amount of turn on some of Warne's deliveries could not physically hurt, but the sheer power could intimidate, without all the psychological ploys he developed over his long career.

Salisbury, the son of a landscape gardener from Northampton, started as a batsman, switching only late in his teens to leg spin. He had to leave his native county when another youngster called Andy Roberts (not *the* Andy Roberts) showed more promise. The county had no need for two such experimental players on its staff. Yet Salisbury, who left school with two O Levels, kept going.

'I was self-taught,' he says. 'I started off with just one good ball every 20. I persevered and bowled and bowled and bowled.

'I was a determined little bugger. My upbringing made me self-sufficient, but also I was determined to prove my worth in the world. That's a good character trait that helped me survive 20-odd years of first-class cricket.'

Salisbury moved to the Lord's ground staff then to Sussex, after all-rounder Colin Wells spotted some potential. He soon eclipsed Andy Clarke as the county's first-choice spinner, although they played together a few times.

'Andy wasn't a big turner of the ball,' says Salisbury. 'It was just more that I could turn it and was younger and I could bat higher. He did really well in one-day cricket. He was very accurate. He was a little bit like Anil Kumble, who didn't turn it very much and had to be very accurate. We were different types of bowler. From the ground staff, I went to Sussex, having spent a year becoming a leg-spinner, and I pretty much got into the side straight away.'

'Salisbury made his entry and did well,' says Clarke. 'He was a better fielder than me, which made it an easier selection. We got on very well and often shared a room on away trips.' Clarke regrets that they did not bowl more together. As Clarrie Grimmett and Bill O'Reilly or Tich Freeman and Father Marriott showed in the 1930s, different types of leggie can prosper in tandem.

Salisbury's debut in 1989 was followed by mediocre figures over the next couple of years. Sussex, sensing more potential than they felt Clarke had shown, stayed patient. Maybe this near-obsolete style could do some damage if reprised and honed. Surprise was, after all, a weapon.

Somerset batsman Peter Roebuck confessed to not having faced a leggie since Robin Hobbs:

> Scrap those obituaries. Leg-spin bowling, long since presumed dead if not buried, is alive and burping… Salisbury will do well to survive cold fingers and banal surfaces.
>
> Say a prayer that he makes it, for leg spin is fun. If this really is an age of cruel scoring, an age of 400 rather than 250, he may survive, for leg spin will be a risk worth taking. Much will depend upon his captain, upon global warming and upon the turn of events in cricket. Perhaps the hour has come for a revival in leg spin. Sceptics will confirm that seeing is believing.

The bowler shared Roebuck's excitement and self-confessed naïvety.

'I had a good leg-spinner and a googly that was hard to pick,' says Salisbury. 'I didn't know how to use the googly. I hadn't had much time. I'd only been doing it for a few years by the time I was in my early 20s. Nobody videoed me. Nobody wanted me to look at how I was bowling and where I was going right or wrong. It was simply "keep going". I didn't know my game.'

One former bowler who did know leg spin was Roly Jenkins, the old Worcestershire and England player who lived until 1995. One day he came on to the pitch during play at Worcester to offer his advice. 'He was screaming at me to not to bowl it flat,' says Salisbury. 'That's how passionate he was.'

In 1992, after a successful tour with the England A team and some good early-season performances, Salisbury was picked for England. Aged 22, he became the first specialist leg-spinner to represent the country in a Test match since Essex's Robin Hobbs in 1971. The press gathered at Hove for interviews and pictures. 'It was like something had dropped from the moon,' says Hobbs.

One of Salisbury's first experiences as an England squad member was not encouraging. Wicketkeeper Jack Russell was unsure of his ability to deal with his variations. 'During the lead-up to that Test match Jack Russell couldn't read my googly,' says Salisbury. 'So he and Alan Knott, who was coaching him, decided to tell me to give Jack a signal. They got me to turn one way at the end of my run-up for the leg-break and the other way for the googly. When I started bowling I was trying to remember which way to turn, on top of the pressure of making my debut. That f***ed me up.'

However, in that first match, against Pakistan, hardly clueless versus spin, he took five wickets. The first was a beautifully flighted leg break to dismiss captain Javed Miandad, caught by Ian Botham, playing in his last Test.

'It was a perfect ball,' says Robin Hobbs. 'Javed Miandad was a world-class player. Salisbury drew him forward and got him caught at slip. I watched on telly and thought, "Goodness me. You've really got something going for you, lad, if you can bowl like that." I couldn't bowl to Miandad when I was in the nets at Glamorgan with him. He hit me all over the park. Salisbury really looked like he had a future.'

Salisbury helped drag England close to victory over a team regarded as one of the most talented in history. His three wickets for 49 in the second innings contributed to getting Pakistan eight down. However, left-hander Wasim Akram hit 45 to win a fascinating contest for the visitors. Salisbury had more than done his bit. As Richie Benaud, the supreme leg-spinner of a previous era, noticed, he seemed to 'have a little bit about him'.

The next match was not a success. Salisbury scored a fifty, but conceded 184 runs for no wicket and was dropped. Still, he ended the English season with 87 first-class wickets, and was named as one of *Wisden*'s Five Cricketers of the Year. The sense of incredulity that England had finally picked a leg-spinner was humorously evoked. 'On that same Thursday morning in June, odd-looking birds with snouts and curly tails were reportedly sighted flying over St John's Wood.' *Wisden* delighted in reporting the doings of Salisbury, 'a south coast anachronism' who was 'blessed with the requisite mix of optimism and realism demanded of one who plies such a precarious trade'.

Salisbury came back for the drubbing by India the following winter. Initially not in the full squad, he went along as a net bowler. The management changed its mind and put him into the Test team.

'I had a horrendous tour,' he says. 'It was January and I was playing for the first time since September. I hadn't played anything in the long form of the game and we were being smashed about by Sachin Tendulkar and Vinod Kambli. There I am playing in India, in front of 100,000 people with nothing to fall back on.' India's leg-spinner Anil Kumble got 21 wickets in the series.

If Salisbury, feted for his rarity, was beginning to feel lonely in his role, the 1993 season worsened the sensation. Ahead of the Ashes, Australian captain Allan Border was asked what he thought of the players he might face. 'England? Impressed by [fast bowler Andy] Caddick,' he replied. 'Also liked the look of Salisbury... If I were picking the England team I'd pick some young players and perhaps be prepared to lose for a couple of seasons. Young players and Gatting. He'd be in my team.'

Mike Gatting, aged 35, made it into the squad for the first Test at Old Trafford. Salisbury did not. It was in this match that a portly, ear-ringed, bleach-haired genius announced himself. Shane Warne's first ball in Ashes cricket, to Gatting, is probably the most-watched in cricket history. It did indeed 'Shane' in sharply through the air to outside leg stump, before 'Warning' away to take out Gatt's off stump. Bemusement turned to amazement. The wicked movement of the ball, repeatedly shown on TV, screamed out the name of its deliverer, 'Shane Warne. Shane Warne. Shane Warne.'

The 'ball of the century' was not a false promise of greatness. Warne followed it up with performance after performance, as the Aussies easily retained the Ashes.

'The problem with most budding leggers is to give them enough bowling to develop their skills – hard for a captain to do if they are going for six an over,' says Ted Dexter, England's chairman of selectors from 1989 to 1993. 'That was where Shane Warne broke the mould. Due to his great strength and spin rotation, he had this marvellous natural dip and swerve in to the right-handers, which was hard to get at. So he always bowled economically, even when he was not taking wickets. Because of this he got to bowl lots of overs and developed quickly as a result.'

As Warne continued to astound, the clamour for leg-spinners to imitate him grew. The prism changed. Salisbury could no longer be viewed as an interesting remnant of a bygone age. He bowled the same way as Warne. Why wasn't he as good?

At the time one wondered what it must be like to be Salisbury. In fact, it evoked thoughts of the theatre. In 1979 the playwright Peter Shaffer produced a work widely regarded as his masterpiece. *Amadeus*, later to become an Oscar-winning film, portrayed the increasingly fanatical jealousy felt by Italian composer Antonio Salieri towards his younger, brilliant rival, Wolfgang Amadeus Mozart. The play's plot was not what really mattered. It was a vehicle to demonstrate a theme of the unjustness of genius.

Salieri was a conscientious but merely talented man. Mozart was transcendentally brilliant. Yet his behaviour was crude and childish. Debauched parties, drinking, sexual innuendo, scatological humour, a girlish giggle. Shaffer's Salieri was outraged that God had chosen such a 'creature' upon whom to bestow his gifts.

The parallel is clear. Salisbury was a decent family man, universally regarded in cricket as a good egg. But the majority of his career played out as Warne, cartoonishly painted in the press as a womaniser, partygoer and junk food gourmet, became the best leg-spinner in history.

Shaffer's Salieri was an imagination. There is little historical evidence to show the composer had such strong feelings about Mozart. The reality is likely to have been more prosaic, an awareness of and wonder at what his rival could do.

Salisbury was more like one imagines the real Salieri to have been than Shaffer's version. Like Salieri, whose surname sounds a little similar to his own, Salisbury had the misfortune to share his time with a one-off.

Warne glided into position at the crease, releasing accurate, energy-filled sizzlers to confuse even the shrewdest international batsmen. He was all purpose – and, indeed, 'all-purpose'. He could take wickets *and* dry up runs. One sensed Warne was constantly scheming, but not what his plan consisted of. He had control of himself and the situation.

The young Salisbury did not appear to have the same technical self-assurance. He trotted up six paces, his blond hair flapping. The arm movement began by his right hip and his hand came through high.

If Warne flowed into an explosive effort, Salisbury had to work hard to make his bowling repeatedly accurate for Test cricket, let alone subtle and deadly enough to get top international batsmen out.

Salisbury managed seven wickets in the away series against the still near-great West Indies in 1994, featuring a rampant Brian Lara. Thereafter it got worse and worse. In his last eight Tests, stretched over four years from 1996 to 2000, he took five wickets. Each success became an event, not an expectation.

He was dropped after the West Indies series, came back against Pakistan in 1996 and was dropped again. For a couple of winters after that, Salisbury went to Australia to play Grade cricket, where the tradition of leg spin was stronger than in modern county cricket. 'They had an understanding of leg spin,' says Salisbury. 'They had a real love for it and realised the value. In England you've got to be a very good leg-spin bowler to survive. That goes back to the value people place on it and the time they are willing to dedicate to seeing it prosper.'

Terry Jenner, Warne's mentor, passed on some tips. One was to give the ball more air, an echo of Roly Jenkins's intervention at Worcester a few years before. Salisbury even had a one-to-one with Warne himself.

Another thing Salisbury noticed in Australia, something he has in common with several other leg-spinners I have spoken to, was that it was easier to bowl with the Kookaburra ball used there than the Dukes used in England. It had better grip, felt like a nicer, rounder shape in the hand and was less slippery. According to Salisbury and others, including Warne, who had a few problems with the Dukes himself, the Kookaburra is more conducive to accurate leg-spinning.

By the start of 1998, infused with new ideas, Salisbury felt ready for another crack at Tests, but, when talking to the press, offered a defensive, almost prophesying caveat, 'It is a difficult art. A lot can go wrong. You can get it a centimetre wrong in your action and it affects it by two yards at the other end.'

Hope turned to hurt, once again, as, at Trent Bridge, South Africa's Hansie Cronje launched a premeditated assault. The humiliation worsened in the next match, at Headingley, when the crowd began *that* chant, 'You're worse than David Beckham. You're worse than David Beckham.'

'I think I was treated particularly harshly,' says Salisbury. 'That stuff scars you but you have to cope with it.'

Salisbury also feels he was the victim of a feud between two very different cricket correspondents. One was Christopher Martin-Jenkins, then of the *Daily Telegraph* – an unabashed supporter. A Sussex man and a romantic, he constantly pushed for Salisbury's inclusion in the England XI.

'He loved watching me, a Sussex bowler who was a blond, bouncy-haired leg-spinner,' says Salisbury. 'At the time he probably built me up a bit too much. He was very pro-myself. He was a wonderful man.'

Before the South Africa series in 1998 Martin-Jenkins pushed the case for Salisbury's inclusion, arguing that even if he was 'no Warne or Mushtaq, it would be very surprising if, given the chance, he were not to outbowl Paul Adams', the visiting team's left-arm googly bowler, with a famed 'frog-in-a-blender' action.

Martin-Jenkins's rival was Michael Henderson of *The Times*. He was more hard-headed and anti-Establishment in his views than Martin-Jenkins. The two did not get on. They differed sometimes, it seemed, to spite each other.

'I think there was a battle between those two and I was at the centre of it,' says Salisbury. 'Henderson wrote some horrendous stuff about me. He was just being the Antichrist to CMJ. He's a superb writer, but I don't particularly like the person. It's not romantic; it's sarcastic. He took it upon himself to abuse and demean me. Part of my character is I actually care about what people think about me.'

Always readable, some of Henderson's remarks were back-of-the-sofa stuff. 'The Thames will freeze over before Salisbury becomes the bowler people want him to be,' he wrote in one piece, 'and it is in everybody's interest to acknowledge that now before the lad becomes a complete laughing stock. Salisbury is here under false pretences and he can now go back to tending his allotment, or painting fences, or whatever it is he does.'

Salisbury was retained for the one-off Oval Test against Sri Lanka. The freakish Muttiah Muralitharan took 16 wickets on a pitch helpful to his sharp-spinning off breaks. Salisbury, England's sole spinner, got just one wicket – number 11 Murali himself – for 86 runs.

Salisbury slunk back to Sydney, saying, 'I've improved again this summer. Maybe not at international level, but that is something to work on. I'm not going to give up, much as some people have suggested I should.'

There was more comfort at home. In 1997 Salisbury joined an exodus of players from faction-ridden Sussex, moving to Surrey. The county of Tony Lock and Jim Laker once more had a spin pairing to envy, as Salisbury and Pakistan's Saqlain Mushtaq, credited with inventing the doosra, the off-spinner's away turner. They helped power Surrey to three championships. Salisbury tasted success. Under the inclusive, welcoming captaincy of Adam Hollioake he looked happy.

Hollioake has since explained his methods. 'One thing I did with Ian Salisbury was take away the fear,' he said. 'He did worry about going for runs. He didn't really like it. He always had one eye on his runs column. When I brought him on I used to say, "Look, I don't care if you go for runs. I just want wickets." I tried to ease his mind so he could just concentrate on taking wickets.'

If this attitude appears very un-English, it was. Hollioake was raised in Australia, where the handling of leg-spinners was a skill more often used. Salisbury felt loved.

Unlike Eric Hollies, who had to be cajoled into playing for England in that famous last Ashes Test of 1948, Salisbury worked hard to get back into the side. His county form good, England picked him again for the away series in Pakistan in 2000. He took one wicket in three Tests. The series, which England won, incidentally, ended Salisbury's international career.

For once, he complained, railing against the lack of understanding he had received in an English cricketing culture devoted to conformity and containment. Captain Nasser Hussain was criticised. 'I was not given the chance to perform in a pressure situation,' said Salisbury. 'Sometimes in those situations when you have to perform that's when you come to the party. I was so desperate to do well I put a lot of pressure on myself.' Ironically, Hussain had been an outstanding leg-spinner as a schoolboy, but he had lost his action during a growth spurt and turned to batting instead.

One of Hussain's predecessors as captain, Mike Gatting – the man whose wicket had propelled Warne to stardom and who did not get on with Hussain – was sympathetic. 'I can't believe the fields Salisbury has asked for, or been given, in this series,' he said. 'The England captain may believe he is being kind by posting men deep on both sides of the wicket to protect his spinner when he drops short. But you are basically telling the opposition that either the bowler has no confidence in his own ability, or the captain doesn't, or possibly both. That's cruel.'

Henderson was on Salisbury's case again, making a comment still admired today by connoisseurs of acerbic put-downs. 'Confidence means everything in this game. Salisbury, poor lad, has none,' he wrote.

'It was always asking a lot of him to make the leap that everybody in their heart of hearts knew was beyond this modest wrist-spinner, and there was something rather pathetic about the way his team-mates congratulated him on his wicket yesterday. It was as if a backward child had suddenly learned how to spell his name and deserved a treat.'

Yet Salisbury continued to enjoy himself at Surrey until, by 2003, his knee needed a major operation. 'It was completely buggered,' he says. 'I had played a couple of summers with it but I couldn't go on any longer. Trying to avoid the pain had got me into bad habits before the operation, as I tried to take pressure off the knee. But, like I said, I was a determined little bugger and I was ready to come back.'

Salisbury worked with his old Sussex team-mate Peter Moores, who was by then coaching the south coast county. The pair were always close, Moores being godfather to Salisbury's children. Their collaboration prospered to the extent that Salisbury felt he had been rebuilt as an effective leg-spinner.

It was in marked contrast to his early career. 'That sort of coaching I never got when I was young,' he says. 'When I first played for England, aged 22, I just did it raw. It was only my fourth season in first-class cricket. I didn't know what I was doing. I roughly knew where the ball would need to go if I was going to get a wicket and that was it.

'It would have been good to have that self-knowledge that I developed 15 years earlier. I would love to rewind and be able to talk myself through my career, because I back myself to be a very good coach now.'

In 2008 Salisbury moved to Warwickshire and had a successful final year, taking 31 first-class wickets at 27.90. He retired at the end of the season, aged 38, despite feeling as good as he had ever done about his ability to bowl and his knowledge of the technique involved.

His first-class career brought 884 wickets at an average of 32.65. This was better than any leg-spinner in England since Robin Hobbs. However, his Test career was a different story. His 20 wickets in 15 Tests came at an average of 76.95. Judgement of Salisbury in the years since has frequently been harsh.

Mike Atherton, like Hussain, a more-than-decent part-time leggie himself during his youth, added his opinion in his autobiography. 'Warne had the full armoury; it always amazed me, in contrast, that after a career as a professional leg-spinner, Ian Salisbury never added a flipper to his repertoire. It was like being a fast bowler without a bouncer.'

Was this fair? Leg spin requires two basic assets: skill and confidence. Bowling flippers, with a sort of under-flick of the ball to make it skid through low while looking like a conventional leg break, requires vast quantities of both. Salisbury was already struggling in Tests without attempting the flipper. Richie Benaud, one of the greats, took years before he dared try it in a match. Even Warne took a while to master it.

Hobbs thinks Atherton's comments about Salisbury were wrong. 'What a ridiculous thing to say,' he fumes, 'when every wicket Warne got in his 40 during the 2005 Ashes was a leg break.' He has a point. Most wickets for Warne that summer came through variations in the amount of spin, the old campaigner by then relying on his mind as much as his physical gifts.

Salisbury realises the enduring brilliance of Warne, but looks back sadly on the different level of support the two of them received from their respective national set-ups. At one stage early in his Test career Warne's bowling average was 335.

'He had a rickety start and they stuck with him,' he says. 'Then he came to England in 1993. He was in a very good side and proved his value. They improved together, whereas England at the time were getting spanked by the Australians and changing the side.'

So, how good does he think he could have been given an even chance? 'I had a better googly than Shane Warne,' he answers. 'I didn't have the raw talent to be as good as Shane Warne but I could have been 50 per cent better than I was, and therefore closer to him. With all the right treatment and coaching and support, if I had been two-thirds as good as Shane Warne, that's about 500 Test wickets. But I ended up being a tenth of what he was. He was nurtured. Why was he given all that? Why did that happen? The culture, the environment and the time.'

Salisbury makes a comparison between himself and Stuart MacGill, Warne's less accurate and cunning but almost equally effective understudy. 'His record was outstanding,' he says. 'I would say he was better but I won't say there was much difference in ability. He played 44 Tests and took 208 wickets.'

He may not have joined the list of Test greats, yet Salisbury has no need to be ashamed. At Test level, the 'basics' have to be so ingrained that they require no thought. This never happened, because the guidance given to Warne and MacGill to ensure everything was in place was not available. And unlike the previous, largely autodidactic heroes of Australia – Clarrie Grimmett, Bill O'Reilly, Herbert Hordern and Arthur Mailey – Salisbury had not had the time and space to develop his own way of doing things as he would have liked. The grind of county cricket from a young age, with little opportunity for fruitful – rather than rushed and negative – introspection, made this so.

To bowl top-class leg spin the mind must be free enough of technical considerations to scheme, not simply to operate the body. In Tests it cannot be otherwise if one is to survive. I watched Salisbury for much of his golden summer of 1992 and there were few signs of the sort of inaccuracy attributed to him by his critics. The idea that he 'bowled a four ball every over' still rankles. His run rate in Tests was 3.70 per over.

Salisbury later became coach of Surrey but was sacked along with director of cricket Chris Adams in 2013. These days he helps train spinners for young England teams and is looking for full-time work. 'I know what it's like,' he says. 'I've been there and got the T-shirt. Sometimes the best players don't make the best coaches because they don't know how they did it. Everybody's different. That goes for leg spin as well.'

Salisbury says he would like to spend the rest of his professional life helping young leggies, giving them the help he did not receive. English cricket should hope he gets that chance.

Comeback Kid

'He's got a survival thing in him. He didn't trust people much.'

Ian Salisbury on Chris Schofield

B EING the 'next big thing' is never easy. Chris Schofield had the misfortune to have this label attached just as English cricket made its final move towards total focus on the national team.

The Lancashire leg-spinner, aged 21, was named in 2000 as one of the first 12 players to get an ECB central contract. Having taken just over 50 first-class wickets, he joined the likes of Mike Atherton, Alec Stewart, Darren Gough and Graham Thorpe. The squad, under coach Duncan Fletcher, was to become more separate from county cricket. Players would be rested, with time to refine their technique.

Schofield's fellow Lancastrian, former England coach David Lloyd, had considered giving him a debut towards the end of the 1998/99 Ashes, in which Australia's Stuart MacGill took 27 wickets.

It did not happen. While in Australia, however, Schofield was taking part in a net session at Melbourne when Adbul Qadir turned up at the ground. He reportedly declined to approach the Pakistani master for advice. Maybe it was shyness, or maybe the young man felt he did not have anything to learn.

Schofield continued to show promise for Lancashire, chipping in with a few runs in the lower middle order. The England and Wales Cricket Board's new mission to improve selectorial consistency bought him a place in the system.

When the squad for the 2000 series against Zimbabwe was announced, his name was a given. In the first match at Lord's he did not get a bowl, as England easily defeated their opponents inside four days. He got a duck in England's one innings.

In the second, drawn match at Trent Bridge, he hit 57 in the first innings and got a bowl. Schofield's 18 overs went for 73 runs and he was wicketless. That was the end of his Test career.

England's contract system was credited with enabling a freshened, united team to beat the declining but still formidable West Indies later that summer and to move up the world rankings, only Australia truly outclassing them over the next few years. Schofield was not to be a part of any of it.

He returned to Lancashire where, according to colleagues, he was upset at having been dropped after so brief a Test try-out. Coaches said he was unwilling to listen to advice and reluctant to devote adequate time to practice. He was acquiring a reputation for being difficult. Sri Lankan off-spinner Muttiah Muralitharan, later to become the leading wicket-taker in Test history, played for Lancashire in 2001, limiting Schofield's chances. Left-arm spinner Gary Keedy was also a regular.

By 2004 Schofield was on the fringes of the first team, sometimes playing solely as a batsman. At the end of the season, Lancashire released him. Coach Mike Watkinson remarked that he had 'perhaps not reached his full potential'.

In little more than four years Schofield had gone from being an England star of the future to a county has-been. His career looked over. Except Schofield himself did not see it that way. He complained that Lancashire had told him far too late in the season that he was no longer wanted, making it impossible to join another county in time for the following year.

He sued the club for unfair dismissal. Watkinson told an employment tribunal in Manchester that other counties would not have been interested in signing Schofield even if he had been on the market earlier. But, under contract rules, counties were meant to appraise their players throughout the season, informing them of areas to improve and any decisions regarding their future. Schofield argued this had not happened. Yet Lancashire claimed that if they had issued verbal warnings these would have impeded Schofield's performances even further.

Schofield won his case in late spring 2005 and received a pay-out from his former employers. 'It's been a long six months but I'm pleased they've come to the right decision,' he said. 'We've still got another couple of weeks to wait to see what's going to become of it but hopefully I can get back on with my cricket career now.

'I'm a cricketer first and foremost and I've never wanted to be sat in a court over this. Just last week was the start of the championship and to be not involved in one way or another was very hard. It's been frustrating and difficult for me but hopefully now counties will see I was in the right to do this and an opportunity will arise with one of them.'

Unfortunately cricket does not work like that. His name was damaged. Schofield, at the age of 26, seemed finished. However, his setback brought out a quality not obvious in his more cosseted days: determination. He swallowed his considerable earlier pride and played Minor Counties cricket for Cheshire and Suffolk. He became a cricketing journeyman, often sleeping in his car as he travelled around playing for club sides.

'Unfortunately in my last years at Lancashire people only saw me as an out-and-out batter at number six,' he said. 'I didn't get the ball in my hand. No one wanted to sign me as a batter so I had to go away and find my bowling again.'

Enforced humility did not entail a loss of competitive aggression, according to Robin Hobbs, who saw him play at Suffolk. 'He threw his bat and swore at everybody after he was out one day,' he says. But what is a leg-spinner if lacking fight?

Schofield did painting and decorating work as he sought a return to the first-class game. In 2006 Surrey offered it. He played a few times for the first team and picked up eight wickets. It was in 2007 that he showed how useful a player he could still be, but not in County Championship matches. Schofield had hardly played Twenty20 cricket for Lancashire, but Surrey gave him an extended run in the format. That season he took 17 wickets at just 8.82 runs each. He was the leading wicket-taker in the country at the group stage of the tournament.

'[Captain] Mark Butcher and Surrey have looked after Sals [Ian Salisbury] over the years and know how to deal with leg-spin bowlers and look after them,' said Schofield.

'It's good that they've actually thrown me the ball and given me an opportunity to bowl a lot of overs.'

The prodigy-turned-journeyman-turned-short-form specialist then completed his redemption. England picked Schofield to go to the T20 World Cup in South Africa.

'In cricketing terms, the Chris Schofield story is one of the best stories,' said England's chairman of selectors David Graveney. 'In terms of what's happened to him, the downwards trend that happened having played for England, when he was perhaps too young in hindsight, and with Lancashire, and the way in which he has fought back as an individual, to get his life back together again. It's one of the great stories to be told.'

The player agreed. 'It's been a big rollercoaster for me,' he said. 'To be announced in the [pre-tournament squad of] 30 was fantastic, a big confidence boost, and this is even better. Playing with Cheshire and Suffolk was a fantastic year. I was living up in Littleborough [in Greater Manchester] at the time and did a lot of miles up and down the country. I used a lot of my own money, just savings I had to keep me going.'

He did not disappoint in the tournament, getting two wickets against Zimbabwe and one each against Australia and South Africa. England did not fare well and were knocked out in the group stage.

Surrey extended Schofield's contract by two years. 'I'm really pleased that things are back on track for me now,' he said. 'I have had a lot of uncertain times in my life when I wasn't sure where my cricket was headed but since I joined Surrey last year things have moved forward for me. I love playing cricket here and really look forward to the next couple of years where I hope to help Surrey win some more trophies.'

Team manager Alan Butcher said Schofield had 'repaid the gamble' taken by Surrey and that he hoped the 'fairytale' would continue. 'He has overcome reservations people may have had about him as a person and as a cricketer and shown what you can do when you get your priorities in the right order,' Butcher added.

But the fairytale was not to last. His T20 performance in 2008 was okay, but he only took one wicket in first-class matches, costing 143 runs.

The following year, Ian Salisbury arrived at the Oval as a coach, having retired as a player. 'I had just finished on the back of a really good year at Warwickshire,' he says. 'There were rumours that I could still play. It really unnerved Chris. I was bowling in the nets and it was coming out really well. To help his confidence I had to stop bowling.'

Having just achieved some stability in his career and life Schofield felt vulnerable once more. 'There's this thing,' says Salisbury. 'Some people are coachable but by this stage Chris was uncoachable.' The pair spent hours in the nets trying to instil best practices to make him more accurate. It was not easy.

'He's a stubborn bastard who's done it a certain way,' says Salisbury. 'He's got a survival thing in him. He didn't trust people much. He went back to bad habits. He started coming in a different way and he was not as accurate as he could be. I had to work really hard in building up his trust in me.

'I kept coaching him and he started bowling beautifully. But we played a game in Dubai and he went back to his old ways and he got spanked everywhere. I was gobsmacked. Eventually he tried to come over and talk to me. I just thought I had wasted a month of my life here. It was bad for me. It took a while but I calmed down and we got it back together.'

Schofield never got his seasonal first-class average below 40 again and parted company with Surrey in 2011. He was, and is, a prodigiously talented sportsman. He can hit century breaks at snooker, plays golf off a low handicap and took on multiple world darts champion Phil 'The Power' Taylor in a Surrey dressing room challenge for the county's website and almost won.

But his early experiences appeared to scar him, making him nervous. 'We tried to bowl out Glamorgan on the last day in Cardiff,' says Salisbury. 'He bowled one googly the guy didn't pick. He got swept and he didn't bowl another one. He couldn't let go. He's a survivor and he just didn't trust.'

Like Salisbury, Schofield had little coaching early on in his career and was not sufficiently developed when he made his Test debut. He never properly recovered.

T20 cricket gives one less time to think, allowing the uncertain leg-spinner to get through their overs in quick time. The variations of flight and spin have made it a success in the format. The first-class game needs the same variety, but combined with a patience based on the confidence to probe away ball after ball. In T20 line and length become less sacred as a batsman constantly thinks of ways to hit boundaries and the bowler has to alter his deliveries to maintain an element of surprise.

Australian coach Peter Philpott, who worked with Schofield in 1998/99, saw a lot of potential in him, but feels he was not given enough bowling at first-class level. 'In terms of mental development, first-class and Test cricket is like chess, 50-over cricket is like draughts and T20 is like Snakes and Ladders,' he says.

Schofield's first-class career was a mixture of hubris and mishandling, but Schofield now turns out for the Lashings XI, a high-grade team of former stars, where he is among the top performers. Cricket is fun again. 'He's talented,' says Salisbury. 'He's brilliant still. He can enjoy himself now.'

The victim of a misunderstanding system, or his own worst enemy, at least Schofield can say he showed a level of character rarely seen. He did it his way.

TJ's Turn

*'He kept it all so uncomplicated and easy
for everyone to understand.'*

Paul Lawrence

*'To be told I needed to do this and
that was a bit mind-blowing. I think I
was quite scared.'*

Matthew Gitsham

AUSTRALIA were terrible in the mid-1980s. In 1985 and
1986/87 England walloped them, leaving captain Allan
Border and his team looking impotent. David Gower,
Mike Gatting (who would not meet Shane Warne for almost a
decade), John Emburey, Phil Edmonds, Ian Botham, Chris Broad,
Tim Robinson, Phil DeFreitas, Allan Lamb. The names bring a
nostalgic pang for a time when England used to beat Australia
with style – and enjoy a few beers after close of play.

By the late 1980s, the Aussies were getting sick of being
thrashed. Border, previously as happy to muck about on the
field with Gower and Botham as with his own men, toughened
up. He returned to England in 1989 on a mission. Having been
humiliated twice as leader, he wanted to win back the Ashes.
Border banned fraternising with the opposition as the Aussies,

with a team including youngsters Dean Jones, Steve Waugh and Ian Healy and the more experienced Terry Alderman, Geoff Lawson and David Boon, smashed an under-prepared England 4-0. Giving nothing away, they never looked like losing a match. The hex held by England's charismatic performers was broken. The spirit of the good old Aussie battler was back.

Behind the scenes, something more subtle was going on. A cricketing culture that had in the past eschewed English-style coaching as a creator of dull orthodoxy, quelling the mongrel spirit in the souls of the young, needed change. Embracing the mores of other sports like athletics and swimming, Australian cricket got serious about raising its standards. Elite players needed elite coaching and monitoring.

So the Australian Cricket Board set up an academy. It started searching for students.

Among the academy's early intakes was a portly young man from the suburbs of Melbourne, boasting little academic achievement and possessing a laissez-faire attitude to his career. This young man, however, had a talent. He could turn the ball – miles. His name was Shane Warne.

The problem was that the men running the academy were old-fashioned types. The sort who wanted hard work from people picked out as potential international cricketers. Students did gym work, took runs along the beach and attended lectures on what it means to represent one's country. They were to be, in a sense, institutionalised: their desire to succeed married to corporate appearance, neatness, conformity.

This wasn't Warne's bag. He liked a beer or 12, pizzas, chasing skirt, flash cars, or at least souped-up bangers in those less affluent days. He and the powers that be clashed. Unless Warne's ability could be utilised properly, there was a danger it would go to waste.

As the writer Gideon Haigh has remarked, had Warne been born a few years earlier than 1969, he might never have prospered. Without the academy system in place, even a gift like his might have gone unnoticed. The other reason is that Terry Jenner, the man described as his mentor, would have been in jail.

Jenner was a remarkable man. Growing up in Western Australia, the son of a shopkeeper, he first learned of leg spin by reading tips on it by former Australian all-rounder Keith Miller in an old magazine.

Jenner had a troubled relationship with father. He was not shown much love. 'If dad was proud of my achievements he never let me know,' he said. 'Every boy wants to be close to his father. But as hard as I tried, mine wouldn't let me. I so desperately wanted to be made to feel that I was worthwhile.'

His parents divorced and he left school at 15. He practised leg spin daily with a friend, but still stuck to his main skill, which was wicketkeeping. This changed when his ability was spotted in the nets during a coaching clinic at Perth's WACA ground and he was persuaded to move to bowling full-time.

Jenner gained an early taste of fame in 1962/63 when, aged 18, he bowled visiting England captain Ted Dexter in the nets at the WACA with a googly. 'Maybe I let him,' jokes Dexter when asked about the incident. Yet Jenner's usual contact with the English game was not as enjoyable. Tony Lock, the left-arm spinner who had partnered off-spinner Jim Laker during Surrey's glory years, was now based in Western Australia and captained the state side.

Jenner remembered that Lock had 'had little to do with coaching a young spinner. And coming from England where leg spin had for years been unfashionable, he had little idea about wrist-spinning and how they should go about it.' There was also a suspicion that Lock was holding him back to hang on to his own place in the side. Unable to get enough matches, Jenner moved to South Australia.

He prospered there and played in nine Test matches, never securing a permanent place but ending with a respectable average of 31.20. Jenner retired in 1976. After that his troubles began in earnest.

Jenner became addicted to gambling and was found guilty in 1988 of stealing money from his employer to pay off debts. He was sentenced to six and a half years in jail, serving 18 months.

In his remarks, the judge referred to Jenner as a 'parasite'. For a man with low self-esteem this was doubly painful.

Ian Chappell, Jenner's former Test and state captain, is another remarkable man. A granite exterior is coupled with a probing mind and an immensely strong desire to fight for a cause. In recent years he has campaigned for what he sees as unfair treatment of asylum seekers by the Australian authorities. They should, he reasons, get a fair go. After all, all they want is to create a better life than is possible in a festering hell-hole of corruption, poverty and disease. If they choose to risk their lives crossing the ocean on craft barely capable of navigating a pond, then it is an injustice to lock them up in facilities in northern Queensland when they arrive, he reasons.

When Jenner was released from prison, few people wanted to know him. Even if they did, they could not override their embarrassment. Chappell was different. He believed Jenner, still on parole, deserved a chance.

He backed Jenner, telling him to face the world again, despite his overwhelming urge to hide from it. And, he reminded Jenner, he had a skill. He had been a leg-spin bowler for Australia, for God's sake. Use it, he told him.

Chappell did Jenner another favour. He recommended him to the founders of the Australian academy, where his expertise might be useful.

'There weren't many better qualified to speak on the subject of wrist-spin bowling than TJ,' said Chappell, 'and he was a fierce protector of the art. He understood the art and its practitioners and, most importantly, was able to communicate his thoughts clearly and concisely, at times with a brutal frankness that typified the man.'

Warne and Jenner converged at the academy, one in need of guidance from someone with whom he could empathise, the other in desperate need of self-worth. If Warne was to succeed under his tutelage it would be the ultimate win-win situation.

'With our first handshake, there was an immediate affinity,' Jenner remembered.

Warne, always wanting to be seen as cool, once likened himself to the Fonz, from the nostalgic American sitcom *Happy Days*. The Fonz, essentially morally correct, was the type who hated taking diktats from those in authority, their status apparently resting on position rather than achievement. Warne felt the same. An ex-con who liked a beer and had bowled leg spin for Australia was more to his liking than a bunch of people he saw as stuffed shirts.

'Everybody knows the trouble with "do-this, do-that",' Warne reminisced, in an unconscious echo of the remarks Aubrey Faulkner had made when outlining his own thoughts of over-regimented English coaching during the 1920s. 'When you are being told what to do all the time it becomes hard and sometimes you rebel. It helped that Jenner was capable of doing everything that he suggested to me.'

Warne dwelt on the word 'suggested', in contrast with the 'over-strict regime' of the academy. It was 'refreshing to meet somebody who did not impose his methods on me. He would plant an idea in my mind, but never complain if I couldn't do it. It was always "Keep going, try harder, you'll get there" – and encouragement like that picks you up.'

Warne's talent was obvious to Jenner and they worked well together. Unfortunately, he still detested being at the academy. Jenner, his 'brutal frankness' intact, was not afraid of administering a rollicking or two to someone he still feared could ruin his life, just like he had. However, Warne misbehaved one time too many and became the first, and only, member of the academy to be expelled.

Such ability could not be resisted, though, and Warne, despite his lack of dietary and disciplinary rigour, started to make it. He played for Victoria and, based on promise rather than performance, he got picked for Australia. Jenner remained his coach, picking up on imperfections where they occurred. Warne felt able to take it from Jenner.

His start in Tests was difficult, getting smashed around by India. But by the start of the 1993 Ashes series Warne had helped win matches against Sri Lanka, New Zealand and the West Indies.

Yet the brilliance of 'that ball' to Mike Gatting – the first delivery of his Ashes career – surprised everyone. The expert bespoke coaching available at the academy had, surely, helped its most recalcitrant pupil.

In the autumn of 1993 England coach Micky Stewart invited the former Australian leg-spinner and coach Peter Philpott, co-founder of the Spin Australia programme to find and nurture talented youngsters, to speak at a seminar for coaches in Lilleshall, in the East Midlands. There was a welcoming atmosphere. England were desperate to get back to winning ways, even if it meant copying Australia. This included leg spin. Philpott knew why. 'The 1993 series between England and Australia was a culmination of this growing movement,' he wrote. 'The performance of Shane Warne on that tour did more for wrist-spinning than 30-odd years of coaching could have done.' Don Bradman felt so moved by Warne's success that he wrote to Philpott to say it was good to see a leg-spinner doing well and getting a good bowl.

By the mid-to-late-1990s English batsmen were terrified of Warne. He could turn it feet, land it accurately and out-think players. This was not to mention the use of deliveries like the flipper and the slider, which frequently made them look stupid.

Not only this but, whenever Warne was injured, another leg-spinner, almost as good, took his place. New South Wales's Stuart MacGill, an intellectually inquisitive wine connoisseur, spun the ball even further. He lacked Warne's subtlety, accuracy and drift but he was, without doubt, world-class, taking 27 wickets as Australia cruised to another victory in the 1998/99 Ashes. They were both winning Test matches, including – in Warne's case – in England. All the old talk about English pitches being too slow for leggies to prosper appeared little more than hokum when top performers were around. In county cricket, India's Anil Kumble and Pakistan's Mushtaq Ahmed took 105 and 95 wickets respectively in 1995.

By the mid-1990s English pitches had been covered outside the hours of play and during rain intervals for almost three decades. This effectively ended the occurrence of sticky wickets after rain, which had turned off-spinners and slow left-armers into occasional world-beaters for the previous century or more.

Some advocated a return to uncovered pitches in the belief that this might help leg-spinners. 'This is often suggested as a recipe for helping English cricket. I say codswallop,' wrote an unsympathetic Ian Chappell in 1994. 'Uncovered pitches at first-class level would encourage the expectancy of easy pickings for the bowlers. Leg-spinners are the antithesis of easy pickings.' He was right. The whole point of leg spin was that its inherent power, when it was done with a full use of the wrist, could overcome the hindrance of all but the deadest pitches. Other styles could not create magic balls on unresponsive surfaces. As English pitches had become more uniform and less prone to early deterioration, this was precisely when leg spin should have regained its ascendancy, but the indigenous culture to nurture it no longer existed.

Since 1993 all County Championship matches have been scheduled for four days, meaning there is less onus on a quick result and early deformation of surfaces than before. Logically, that should disadvantage off-spinners and slow left-armers more than leggies. That said, the relative uniformity of pitches came with a general lack of bounce, unwelcome to conventional leg-spinners, who tend to bowl with more overspin, and therefore dip through the air, than off-spinners because of the extra flexibility of the wrist allowed by the style.

But, then again, too much bounce can be detrimental too. Peter Philpott has written that it can 'become a problem as well as a strength' in Australia, as the ball can jump so high that bowled or LBW dismissals are unlikely. Much of the success of Sussex's Pakistani import Mushtaq Ahmed in the 2000s came because he was small and able to skid the ball along on the flat pitches at Hove. Much of the reason for Clarrie Grimmett's development of a flipper, which became so successful in England, in the 1920s was to overcome excessive bounce in Australia. In the 1950s Richie Benaud produced a leg break with only side spin, and no dip, for similar reasons. Leg spin comes in many guises. That is why it should be near-universal rather than a rarity, with the right brains in place.

Chris Wood, the ECB's pitches consultant, says county surfaces became a little 'samey' by the 1990s. He is working on an experiment at Loughborough University to create pitches that offer more bounce than usual English conditions, by testing various combinations of clay, sand and other soil components. It is his aim to ensure wear towards the end of a match without excessive deadening from soil break-up. This, he reasons, should bring more leg-spinners in to county cricket. Wood is studying in particular the surfaces on offer at Old Trafford, which are harder than most in England and more abrasive, allowing leg-spinners greater purchase on the ball. The development is welcome, if belated, but attitudes, not pitches, are the true enemy.

That is not to say that nothing was done in the 1990s. As the decade went on, English cricket realised it needed a system to create leg-spinners. If Aubrey Faulkner had started a cottage industry in his indoor school in the 1920s, the England and Wales Cricket Board wanted to build a factory.

In spring 1999, almost six years after Peter Philpott's lecture, the ECB – under the leadership of Lord MacLaurin, former chairman of the supermarket chain Tesco – set out a series of goals. Foremost was for England to become the best Test nation by 2007 and to win the World Cup in that year. A less well remembered part of MacLaurin's plan was for England to have a leg-spinner playing regularly in Tests by then. Part-funded by the Brian Johnston Memorial Trust, the ECB set up the Wrist-Spin Development Programme. It looked to harness the interest shown by youngsters in this style since the advent of Warne. The ECB worried that there had still been no breakthrough in the professional, particularly the international, game.

Who better to provide this than the man who had given the world Shane Warne? The ECB's performance director, former Test opener Hugh Morris, approached Jenner and he was soon on his way to England.

This was a decade after his release from prison, a decade during which he had seen his reputation restored and coaches around the world had increasingly started asking for his help. Paid a hefty sum by the ECB, he established a scouting programme. The country was divided into zones and youngsters were called to trials and given help at centres of excellence, with the likes of Robin Hobbs and Warwick Tidy helping out. Up to 140 boys and girls attended trials in February and March 2000 and were eventually whittled down to two or three who were to spend time with Jenner in Adelaide the following autumn, staying with him in his bungalow and imbibing all there was to know about the culture of Aussie leg spin.

Jenner, in a state of optimism, thought his efforts would prevent the need for affirmative action by the ECB, saying:

> Our aim is to have a leg-spinner play for England by 2007 purely on merit.
>
> That means we'll need seven or eight playing county cricket by then, which means we need to get boys bowling leg spin in under-14 and under-15 cricket now.
>
> Shane's always done very well over here, so has Abdul Qadir, while Ian Salisbury's an effective county bowler but couldn't defend himself at Test level. Once you find someone who can, you'll have a match-winning option that you've lacked for many years.
>
> Believe me, the interest is out there amongst young boys, but when Shane first toured England in 1993 the TCCB, as it was then, had no programme to harness the interest in leg spin that he created. This time the ECB have.

Jenner worked on getting coaches to understand leg spin through a process of demystification. He promoted a step-by-step method of achieving a reliable technique. Bowlers went through a series of drills, involving grooving their action from a standing start. The theory was that this was the best way to get perfectly side-on, maximising the pivot around the front leg and the explosive power and accuracy achievable.

There was a five-point plan:

- Align the shoulders and hips toward the target
- Lead with the front arm toward the target. Pull it down
- Bowl 'up and over' with the shoulders
- Pivot-rotate the shoulders 180 degrees
- Complete the action with the bowling shoulder facing the target, with the bowling hand at the left hip and the front arm sticking 'out the back'

Jenner's assistant coach Paul Lawrence remains in awe. 'He kept it all so uncomplicated and easy for everyone to understand,' he says. 'The drills he did, everything was designed to make it seem like common sense. He was brilliant.

'TJ had an incredible memory for actions. You would be running a session and he would say, "You never used to do that. What happened?" He just believed so much in making sure that you got the action right from delivery stride and building it back so that you got a run-up and approach that suited your action and not the other way around.

'There's bowling spin and there's being able to really, really bowl. Shane Warne was a once-in-a-lifetime bowler, but you get others who can spin it well.'

The action-based, rather than run-up-based, approach reached its apogee in Warne by his late career, when he did little more than walk to the wicket before bowling.

One of Jenner's first charges was Matthew Gitsham, the son of a bank manager from Bridgwater, Somerset. He started leg-spinning by watching the overseas Australian professional at his club nets and mimicking his action. This had gone unaltered until he arrived in Adelaide.

Jenner took Gitsham to the nets in parks and the combined indoor cricket and netball centre near his house in the suburb of Brighton. 'As far as I was concerned, it was going well and I was quite happy when I got there,' Gitsham recalls. 'But TJ told me there were a few things in my action that were quite bad and I hadn't realised. I had been quite a happy-go-lucky fellow. I had been thinking I was going pretty well. To be told I needed to do this and that was a bit mind-blowing. I think I was quite scared as a young lad. He was quite an abrupt fella and I was probably a little bit timid.'

Gitsham was told to keep a diary of his progress. The drills continued. 'TJ was standing behind you,' he says. 'You would bowl one ball and look round to see what he said about it. Generally people were just looking for praise from him, but he wasn't the most generous praiser in the world. To get praise from him meant something.'

After two weeks it was time to return to England and keep practising the drills, but without any further input from Jenner for the time being.

'I had forgotten my old action,' says Gitsham. 'I didn't really have an action. I had broken it down so much I had forgotten to run up and bowl. Somerset lost a little bit of interest.'

Gitsham returned to Adelaide the following winter, but in the intervening months his bowling had worsened and he felt confused. Eventually he gave up serious cricket and instead went to Plymouth University to study sports science.

'After I graduated, I thought I should give cricket a bit of a go again,' he says. 'I thought I owed it to myself and TJ. I paid off my own bat to go back out there. I put everything into it. I found an action through sheer hard work. Eventually I managed to combine the action with my delivery stride and my run-up. It was well worth it because the end product was hugely better than when I was 16 or 17. I had spent many hours doing it.'

Jenner used an unorthodox method to complete the work of improving Gitsham's understanding of leg spin, by asking him to help with coaching.

The Australian was not averse to making some money on the side and had agreed to give personal tuition to a 36-year-old Indian office worker from the United Arab Emirates who, while being an undistinguished player, harboured a quaintly naïve ambition to play Test cricket alongside Sachin Tendulkar and Anil Kumble.

'He wasn't the most talented of people, but he got better,' says Gitsham. 'I got him into a side-on action. Eventually he was spinning the ball a little bit. TJ asked me to go and help teach him for a couple of weeks. Improving his action and having to explain things to him, I completely got what TJ had been trying to explain to me. It just clicked.

'I spent three months with TJ, working three or four hours a day, and by the time I went back to England, I was bowling as well as I ever had, far better than when I had gone out there for the first time. When I went back I knew exactly what I was trying to achieve.'

Jenner had effectively stripped Gitsham down and rebuilt him, while delivering a lesson in self-reliance. It was a process one could hardly have expected Gitsham to complete in the time allowed by the ECB's scheme and the constraints of the busy English summer. Gitsham's extra dedication and time out of the English system paid off.

Under Jenner's tutelage he trained hard and, having been castigated like a young Warne for not looking after himself, lost 15kg during his stint in Adelaide. After returning to England he got a few matches for Gloucestershire's second XI and, in 2008, made his debut for the first team.

Jenner was delighted, saying, 'I feel it is naïve to think a spinner will mature in his teens. Shane Warne certainly didn't. If Matthew Gitsham doesn't end up as a leg spinner with a hundred or more first-class wickets, it will not mean he has failed. Getting there makes him a success and an inspiration to others.'

Gitsham played only four first-class matches and now runs his own carpet-cleaning firm in Bristol. He has since given up playing recreational cricket, but remains grateful to Jenner and glad that he returned to the game when he thought his chance had passed.

Another of Jenner's early intakes was to prove fruitful. In 2002 Mark Lawson, of Yorkshire, and Michael Munday, of Somerset, were chosen.

Discussing Lawson, shortish of build and slowish of speed, Jenner urged caution and patience. 'I'm worried that people expect too much, parents, coaches, club captains, schools, teachers,' he said. 'They try to get lads to bowl at the economical speed Warne bowls at but they don't look at his build, shape or strength. A lot of people see this slider which is getting Warney a lot of leg befores and say give him one. Why? Warney didn't have one until he was 29. Why should he have one at 17?'

Lawson, with a fierce determination to succeed, as well as a good side-on action, was the first of the scheme's participants to make it to county level, playing for Yorkshire in 2004 against Somerset at the Scarborough festival. He was the first specialist leggie to play for the team in the County Championship since Peter Kippax, later a noted bat-maker, in 1962.

Like his hero Warne, he had his hair streaked blond. 'I suppose I thought I may as well go for the whole package,' he joked.

He praised Jenner and stated, 'I want to be the best I can, to play regularly for Yorkshire and then to play Test cricket. It doesn't matter what you're doing in life, I believe that you have a duty to give of your best.'

Sadly it did not turn out like that, with Yorkshire releasing him in 2008, aged just 22, followed by stints at Derbyshire and Kent. Lawson retired from the professional game and is now a coach.

Paul Lawrence, who was to join Jenner as his assistant coach in 2005, thinks the likes of Lawson and Gitsham benefited hugely from his methods.

'On alignment and approach, TJ tried to give youngsters the basics to work from and give them the best chance of being the best wrist-spinners that they could be,' he says. 'Coaches tend to complicate it or allow bad things to continue happening because they have no understanding of how to coach leg-spinners.

'There was an allowance for individuality in TJ's methods, but basics are needed to be put in place. In order for a bowler to be effective, the action has to be effective as well. I've seen it work and it works and works and works.'

Jenner used to look for leg-spinners he described as having 'the gift' – the ability to bowl spin with power, generating rapid revolutions. One such bowler was Michael Munday, who came to the attention of scouts while a teenager in Cornwall. In 2001 he was chosen to take part in sessions and made it through to the final trial at Lord's, where Jenner got to have a look at him. He had to wait another year to be selected for the trip to Adelaide.

Munday, who started bowling leg breaks to his brother on the driveway of the family home in Truro, received no significant coaching during his early years. He is glad. 'The knowledge a coach can give a talented leg-spinner has the potential to do more harm than good,' he says. 'Every year as a school coach you will have ten people you can coach in batting and you'll get a feel for how things work and don't. Anyone can be coached the forward defence.

'You see someone who can bowl a leg break. You can see a few bad balls. Maybe you can say not to bowl any bad balls. You can start giving bad advice, like maybe bowl faster and not so high to be more accurate. That's dangerous advice.'

Shortly before he was due to begin his studies at Oxford, Munday spent three weeks with Jenner and did some drill work. He impressed the coach. During his first year at university Munday made his first-class debut, Andrew Strauss becoming his first wicket. After graduation, Munday, who had registered with Somerset, went back for three months to Jenner and played some Grade cricket. But he had a mixed relationship with the guru.

'He was very passionate about leg spin and that really came across,' Munday says. 'In terms of his coaching, technically he tried to keep it really simple and get the coaches out there, so they could bring back a couple of things, like being side-on and getting your weight going towards the target.

'TJ thought that was the right way. But you look at someone who's done well like Mushtaq Ahmed and he's quite front-on. There's room for negotiation. He was a little bit black and white, TJ, in terms of "this is the way it works". To Mushtaq Ahmed, he would have said, "Let's get you side-on." He wouldn't have said,

"Actually, you're a pretty good bowler front-on. Let's see how we can enhance that.'"

The drills began to get on Munday's nerves. 'A lot of what he would do with me was stationary. The theory is that it gives you the opportunity to stand side-on and get a feel for that. But as soon as you run up, the chances are you will just get in the position you always used to get in. It's quite hard to train yourself while you're in the run-up.

'When we went to Adelaide for two weeks, we spent a week and a half to 13 days going with just one step. Then we went back to the run-up. What would generally happen then is you wouldn't actually take anything with you that you'd been practising. Clearly if you're playing in a game you are going to have to run up.'

Munday thinks the drills should have been interspersed with practising the run-up, rather than moving towards it over a period of weeks.

Jenner's critics thought he was trying to make all of his charges bowl like Shane Warne. Until the action was perfect, they had to keep refining. Robin Hobbs found Jenner's methods over-prescriptive. 'He had his system. I call it a theatrical act,' he says. 'A lot of things were right about him. He was a very interesting person to listen to, but you had to do it his way. You had to follow what he thought was right. He wouldn't accept you doing it any different. Now, I don't think that's quite right.'

Jenner, a man who had left prison with little self-esteem, had seemingly become convinced his own methods, which had helped him rebuild his life and his reputation, were correct. He started calling himself the 'Spin Doctor', a sobriquet invented by Aussie wicketkeeper Ian Healy, who had watched him working with Warne and getting results. As Warne came to dominate world cricket, some could see in Jenner a fastening of views. Some of his English pupils found there was no longer the lack of a 'do-this, do-that' attitude, which Warne had found so refreshing. The brilliance of Warne and the success of his own methods in enhancing that had apparently created a dogma.

After his three-month stint with Jenner, Munday returned the next year to Adelaide to play club cricket. 'It went very well,' he says. 'By the time I left, at Christmas, I was joint leading wicket-taker with a guy who's now played for Australia – Ryan Harris.

'I didn't stay with TJ. We met up when I went back out there, but I don't think we'd had much contact over the summer. When you talk about him and Warne, you talk about kindred spirits and larrikins. That didn't quite work with us.

'He wasn't prepared to listen. It was more "my way or the highway" type thing. The interesting thing to me is that a lot of people say he tried to get everyone to bowl like Shane Warne. I don't think it's true. I've never seen Warne stand there and do drills. I think he would just walk through one step to get some feeling of momentum. It makes a big difference. If you just stand there you've got no momentum. You have to launch yourself to bowl a good ball.

'I know TJ had some successful sessions with Anil Kumble, where they just worked on a couple of things. I doubt very much he had him just standing still.'

This might be a little unfair, as Warne himself once wrote about the help he received from Jenner when he returned from a finger injury in 1996/97. He felt uncertain and that his deliveries were lacking fizz. Warne recalled that Jenner had 'corrected the matter very simply by getting me to bowl from a standing start and spin the ball purely from my hand. He had noticed from replays during the previous game in Brisbane that I was putting the ball on the spot rather than spinning it there.'

Munday, who left Oxford with a first-class degree, found a lack of understanding at Somerset which, he argues, impeded his career. 'I always felt they were looking for me to be Shane Warne because I spun it big and they wanted me not to bowl any bad balls. To me, if you're spinning it a long way and not bowling any bad balls, that's Warne's level, because that's what he was doing.

'Justin Langer obviously played with Warne a lot and Marcus Trescothick played against him. Every time you bowled a waist-high full toss or something, there would be this thought around, "Warne doesn't do that. You've released the pressure that we're building up," rather than the thought that you might get a wicket next over bowling a good ball. It's almost like to justify your place in county cricket you have to be a potential Test match bowler.'

Munday, like other bowlers on Jenner's scheme, found it harder to hold the ball properly when he returned to England. This was not because of colder conditions but the fact the Dukes ball was used in England. It had more lacquer than the Kookaburra used in Australia. Even Warne reported struggling with it during the Edgbaston Test of 1997, which England won courtesy of a Nasser Hussain double hundred.

In 2007 Munday took 8-55 in the last match of the season as Somerset secured an innings victory over Nottinghamshire. Team-mate Marcus Trescothick was ebullient, predicting he could be the 'x-factor' to help the county win the championship for the first time.

Yet Munday's success came at the wrong time. Just as he was hitting top form the season was over. He struggled in 2008. This continued the next year.

'I probably did worse in 2009 by taking a bit of the influence of Jenner that – if there's a problem – you should look at it technically,' says Munday. 'You can always improve technically or you have a model of what the ideal bowling action is. You want to look for something. You think, "I could be doing this, that or the other," and start wondering how you get rhythm and repeatability.

'It went down that road with negative implications for my action. There was an improvement needed. But there's a question of how I should have gone about it. I had ambitions after 2007 of breaking through. That didn't happen.'

Somerset released Munday at the end of 2010, aged 25. But he kept playing cricket. Liberated from the pressures of the first-class game, Munday is enjoying himself once more. He and fellow Horsham leg-spinner Will Beer, of Sussex, often bowl in tandem at weekends, giving Sussex League crowds a rare treat.

Yet Paul Lawrence thinks the decline of his professional career could have been avoided had he stuck with Jenner's advice. 'In my opinion, what happened was that Michael went away from the drills that he had been doing with TJ because the coach he was working with, and he himself, came to the conclusion that they weren't going to work on those drills anymore,' he says. 'Then Michael, I feel, wasn't the bowler that he had been. He lost all control and bowled too quickly and Somerset dismissed him.'

A good analogy would be a professional musician who deviates from his or her practice, performing fewer scales and so on and becomes less technically proficient. Lawrence feels strongly that Munday was the one who got away. There were some parallels between Jenner and Munday's relationship and that between Aubrey Faulkner and Ian Peebles. In both cases the teacher was concerned that the pupil was moving away from his prescribed methods. Yet there was not the same intensity. After all, Jenner had already tasted huge acclamation for his role with Warne; Faulkner had not created S.F. Barnes. Still, it rankled.

'TJ always spoke about Michael as the one person he thought had the most Warne-like wrist and that ability with his fingers and wrist like Warne,' Lawrence says. 'But he moved away from the drills. I saw him doing it another way and it wasn't working.

'This is where it goes back to what TJ was doing. I've seen it work for players. I know it works. When you get coaches who don't believe in the drills, this is the end result. You can help these players and do drills. But there's so much more that goes into making somebody successful on the pitch at different levels and sometimes it's a little bit of luck as well. All coaches like myself can keep doing is try to pass on the advice from TJ and hopefully it will work and something will come through.'

Munday's predicament was a case of two philosophies clashing in the mind of one very intelligent bowler of limited experience. These were the competing calls to give it a rip, advocated by Jenner, and to keep it tight, demanded by Somerset.

The problem facing leg spin, genuine wristy leg spin of the type offered by Jenner, is essentially one of demand. He and his successors can continue to churn out talented, motivated leg-spinners ad infinitum. But do counties, and their captains, really want them and all they entail? That is the question. Sending a player to Australia to gain an insight into a different culture is good, but returning to one of negativity after a winter away might even be doubly deflating. High hopes can breed bitter disappointment.

Ian Salisbury thinks Jenner's technical influence did little to help Munday, who describes himself as being on the slow side as a spinner, sending the ball down at about 45mph.

'Someone standing still doing drills – if they have no momentum before, then how are they going to be able to do a drill in the right way?' asks Salisbury. 'Yes, Shane Warne could do it. He's immensely strong, but not everyone's like him. If someone needs momentum, if you start doing drills from a standing start, you will make them less potent. Someone like Michael Munday will need momentum to move.'

Salisbury, who has studied the theory of bodily motion, says people can broadly be divided into 'bottom' and 'top' movers. Warne, with his supreme upper-body strength, is firmly of the latter type, not needing much of a run-up. Other bowlers are not.

'Terry Jenner was a passionate enthusiast who also had amazing qualities when it came to bowling the perfect leg-spinner,' says Salisbury. 'He worked in the same way as Shane Warne did. Shane Warne was the perfect spinner. Jenner derived a lot of his thinking from how Shane Warne achieved it. He bowled differently to a lot of other leg-spinners.'

On the videos he posted online, Jenner showed a remarkable facility for delivering the full range of deliveries from a standing start. 'TJ didn't need momentum to be bowling,' says Salisbury. 'He could do it from standing drills. TJ helped Warne very much. For Munday, people would say the ball looked nice but it was too slow and didn't have momentum going towards the batsman. Somerset pitches can be slow too. He turned it but he turned it slowly because he had no momentum.

'This whole Shane Warne thing is brilliant and you thought TJ would inspire a whole generation of leg-spinners around the world. It hasn't quite happened.'

'He found a niche with Warne, thought he was going to make some money, and did,' says Hobbs. 'The ECB thought, "He'll sort our problems out. He'll find somebody. He'll find another Warne." It doesn't work like that. You'll never find another one like him.'

After five years, in 2004, Jenner's coaching had not found any England leg-spinners. Despite his demands for patience, the scheme was changed to focus on the more talented of the youngsters identified by the scouts. The net was cast a little more narrowly as the ECB's self-imposed 2007 deadline for the England Test team to contain a leg-spinner loomed closer.

The ECB's director of spin-bowling coaching, David Parsons, said, 'We are not after "the one" – what is needed is a continual supply of high-quality, talented young wrist-spin bowlers at all levels of the game. Wouldn't it be great if every county had a wrist-spin bowler playing a key role in its first XI? That target too is some way off – but it can be achieved with high-quality guidance, coaching and opportunities at a junior level.'

Even if it fell behind the ECB's arbitrary schedule, some talented players did start getting to county level via Jenner's scheme, Gitsham, Lawson and Munday among them.

Yorkshire, the county which had once decried leg spin, became its temporary spiritual home, in England at least. For, as well as Lawson, the county gave a debut to an outrageously talented leg-spinning all-rounder called Adil Rashid, another of the Jenner boys. The romantics were delighted, not to mention astonished, when Rashid and Lawson bowled in tandem for Yorkshire.

In 2009, Rashid became the first of Jenner's pupils to play for England. During that calendar year he was chosen for five one-day internationals and five T20 matches, but he soon faded away. At least it meant Jenner saw one of his boys reach the big time.

In spring 2010, while in England, he suffered a huge heart attack. Jenner lost lots of weight and never recovered his health.

He died on 25 May 2011 aged 66. Like Aubrey Faulkner more than 80 years earlier, he went just as his efforts looked like showing some long-term results. A large congregation turned out for Jenner's funeral service in Adelaide.

'Terry shared much of himself with everyone he met,' said Parsons, by now the ECB's performance director, 'and I was fortunate to be the recipient of much of this – his fire, his passion, his knowledge, his skills, his humour, his home, his family and his generosity.

'I have memories of Terry that will stay with me forever. He was a wonderfully engaging figure and there can be no doubt that his legacy will live on through the careers of the many coaches and players he inspired and influenced both in this country and overseas.'

Like Faulkner, whose father had been an abusive alcoholic, Jenner had grown up in a messy domestic situation and wanted to help create a better world. In two decades since his release from jail he had righted his wrongs and then some. The scheme set up by the ECB and the constraints on Jenner and his pupils meant it was unlikely to change English cricketing culture in just a few years. The example of Matthew Gitsham showed what might have been and what might still be.

After his death, Jenner's family put out this statement: 'Terry's legacy to spin bowling will live on in all the young spinners and coaches he had the privilege to work with.' They urged his pupils around the world to 'make him proud'. They continue to strive to do so.

Counsellors Of Perfection

'You will clearly know where you want to land the ball and you will be able to concentrate on the task at hand with the complete exclusion of everything else.'

Wording of hypnosis
used on leg-spinner

'Fish and chips.'

Ernie Els

LEG-SPINNERS have never been 'right in the head'. The fine margins between success and failure, the limited number of people who have truly excelled at it, mean it is not a rational career choice for a cricketer.

It has always attracted eccentrics and obsessives. Bernard Bosanquet's experiments, Roly Jenkins's words of advice to a flighted ball: these are but manifestations.

Yet the pain of leg spin can be profound. There are so many variables, so many difficulties, real and imagined. Then there is the deterioration in the culture of English leg spin over the best part of a century. 'It's not easy being me in that dressing room,'

Kevin Pietersen said during a fall-out with the England team in 2012. The words apply equally to English leg-spinners.

One club player felt so helpless in 2005 that he contacted psychologists Jamie Barker and Marc Jones of the University of Staffordshire for help. 'What he was experiencing was a bit like the yips in golf,' says Barker. 'There's this sort of sense in spin bowling that it becomes almost acceptable for a golfer or a spin bowler to develop that syndrome. A lot of golfers I work with say they have got the yips. It's the same with bowlers. They almost create this self-fulfilling prophecy… that I'm going to bowl a bad ball, a full toss or a long hop.'

The old cycle of mistrust was developing. The bowler's captain was starting to lose faith in him, taking him off after a couple of bad balls. His confidence declined.

'I don't think that happens with other bowlers,' says Barker. 'It's a cultural idea that's developed. We see it in football that a coach doesn't like "that sort of player". You get exactly the same sort of thing with a leg-spin bowler. A developing leg-spinner could be nine out of ten one week and three or four out of ten the next. It's a question of whether a team thinks it can afford it. Some of it is down to how a coach or manager wants to develop their squad or team.'

It is not a recently developed phenomenon. In the 1950s Colin Cowdrey, with the sensational Doug Wright in his team, remarked that, when his leg-spinner was having an off day, it felt like being on the field 'with ten men'. It's not very nice feeling like the 11th (non-) man in that situation.

The leg-spinner who approached Barker was having trouble landing the ball properly and his performances were tailing off. He was starting to doubt himself. Most leg-spinners have a similar sensation at some time. Some sportsmen, according to research, react and improve best when given 'instructional' support – reminders of the basic craft behind their previous successes. Others need a proverbial arm around the shoulder, help to deal with their emotions. 'It probably relates to how they developed as children,' says Barker.

COUNSELLORS OF PERFECTION

Barker and Jones devised an eight-week programme to deal with both these needs. They offered remedial coaching for the leg-spinner, taking his action back to basics. The more interesting part of the experiment was what they did to try to heal the mind.

Barker and Jones hypnotised the bowler. The sessions, lasting up to an hour and a half, included giving suggestions such as these during his trance:

- Every time you practise and compete... and when you stand at the end of your run-up your nerves will become stronger and steadier... your mind calmer and clearer... more composed... you will become much less easily worried... much less easily agitated... much less easily fearful and apprehensive... much less easily upset.

- Every time you practise and compete your run-up will be smooth with lots of energy and your bowling action will be tall... you will clearly know where you want to land the ball and you will be able to concentrate on the task at hand with the complete exclusion of everything else.

- And because all these things will begin to happen... exactly as I tell you they will happen... more and more rapidly... powerfully... and completely... with every treatment I give you... you will feel much more confident in both training and competition... particularly when you stand at the start of your run-up ready to bowl.

The idea is that hypnosis changes the way the patient talks to himself when in the pressure situation, achieving what psychologists call 'self-efficacy'.

It is an internalised version of the reassurance Gamini Goonesena remembered getting from fellow leg-spinner Bruce Dooland when things got tough for Nottinghamshire in the 1950s – the sort of support unavailable to this breed of bowler in England today because of its rarity.

After the hypnosis, Barker and Jones offered the bowler technical help with his action, focusing on head position, run-up, arm position and so on. After each coaching session, the bowler watched a video Barker and Jones had compiled of his performances, emphasising the improvement in consistency. He was instructed to watch the tape two hours before each match he played.

The player also used self-hypnosis for ten-minute sessions at home the night before the game, two hours before the start of play and then, just prior to play beginning, in 'a quiet area within a changing room or in a toilet cubicle'.

The self-hypnosis involved taking 100 deep breaths and imagining walking down a flight of stairs. Once at the bottom, they would visualise opening a door, behind which were the thoughts and feelings one wanted to experience during bowling written on laminated cards on a large notice board. Slogans such as 'Be positive', 'Express yourself' and 'Be decisive' were to be imagined.

Once all the cards had been removed, the participant would say to himself, 'Be confident and focused.' He would begin counting upward from one to ten, open his eyes and repeat the phrase before moving from where he was sitting.

Quite what his team-mates queuing for the loo made of this behaviour is anyone's guess. It seemed to have some effect on the bowler, though. His measures of self-confidence improved. His bowling average in the eight matches after the help dropped from 21.3 to 20.5, compared with the eight previous matches. After that it went down to 16.3, suggesting a further degree of self-efficacy, that the help was working more in the longer term. His strike rate improved too.

The study was limited to just one bowler, so resource-intensive were its methods, but it gives a glimpse of the drastic methods English cricket needs to begin healing the psychological wounds inflicted on leg spin.

'Usually we go through most of our lives with support, but when you get into sport, some people can be left to their own devices a bit,' says Barker, echoing the words of Ian Salisbury, Warwick Tidy and many others. Not everyone has the self-reliance of Bill O'Reilly or Clarrie Grimmett. Perhaps today's upbringings do not encourage it, perpetuating the feeling among older cricketers that many of the youngsters have it 'too easy'.

Was it a coincidence that the bowler who turned up asking for psychological help was a leg-spinner? Not according to Barker. Leg-spinners in England do not often hear about the experiences of their fellows, he argues. 'Often they have become *the* spin bowler.' This can raise expectation, more so in these days following the relatively recent retirement of Shane Warne. It must have felt similar when Father Marriott, Doug Wright and, in particular, Ian Peebles were trying in their own ways to follow Sydney Barnes. But at least they, unlike Adil Rashid and Scott Borthwick today, had plenty of co-practitioners to talk to.

'If I worry about what is a highly complicated skill, I'm likely to break down,' says Barker. 'We create quite a lot of stress for players. Expectations become unrealistic. There's a potential for it to become uncontrollable and to see a breakdown of skill.'

So why did Warne, who had built up huge expectations of himself, never buckle in this way? He sometimes remarks that he did not aim at a particular spot when bowling but rather tried to get the ball into such an area as to make the batsman play a specific shot, gradually luring him into a mistake. This runs counter to the late Richie Benaud's dictum that it is best to focus on an exact place on the pitch. Benaud's reasoning was that, if he offered someone several thousand dollars to throw a ball at a target, they would be foolhardy not to aim at it.

Warne was fortunate in having such a naturally strong, repeatable action, made stronger still with the help of Terry Jenner. He was already confident in his mechanics before getting on the field.

'He spoke about how he wanted the batsman to play against him, rather than the spot where he wanted to land the ball,' says Barker. 'That gave him more freedom and helped him to visualise the type of ball he needed. That took the pressure off, saying, "I want this guy to hit me there." If he's hit, he thinks, "Yes, that's where I wanted him to hit me."' It felt like part of a plan, not an uncontrollable pasting.

In a strange way Warne was 'playing the man', something coaches tend to discourage because it can be a distraction from the basic physical task in hand, particularly a repetitive task such as bowling.

Remember that Sydney Barnes had discussed a similar aspect of his bowling many years earlier. At one stage he said his method was to 'always attack the stumps'. On another he said that, like Warne later, he tried to induce certain strokes by moving the ball around. Perhaps this, like a batsman playing strokes in a way to pierce gaps in the field, is the mark of a true master bowler – the 'bossing' of the game.

Warne, by visualising what he wanted to achieve, allowed himself to bowl automatically. 'It's just a very sensible thing to do. It shows a lot of efficacy and belief in himself,' says Barker. 'He doesn't need to think about it.'

Ian Salisbury's problem when he played for England, according to his own analysis, was that he was not technically and mentally 'grooved' into what he was doing. Equally, one of the problems with Jenner's English pupils was that they did not have time to get beyond this focus on the mechanics of bowling before being thrust back into competitive cricket. A few weeks in Adelaide was not enough. In fact, leaving the job started by Jenner unfinished could do more harm than not bothering with him in the first place. Rebuilding takes time.

Trying to perform at the top level of cricket when one's self-efficacy is not fully developed can bring on what has become known as 'paralysis by analysis'. The ultimate aim in sport is to do the basics free of conscious thought, rather like driving a car after a couple of years on the road. This leaves the mind free to scheme about tactics, instead of worrying how to get the ball to land correctly.

'Under higher levels of stress, people begin to regress and start to think about grip and wrist position and the front arm,' says

Barker. 'It clogs the system up and impacts on the signals going to the brain. The more you think about it, the worse it gets. You get to the point where things start to unravel.' Most leg-spinners have been there.

Coaches can add to this when urging leg-spinners not to bowl a 'four ball'. This happened to Michael Munday at Somerset. 'We had a conversation where a coach said, "It's not acceptable for you to bowl a bad ball,"' says Munday. 'I said, "Well, I'm going to sometimes, so where does that leave us?" That just puts it in your head. When I bowl one, what am I thinking? I'm not thinking, "Okay, he's hit that, I'm going to bowl this one higher and spin it." I'm thinking, "I'm going to bowl a slider as fast as I can at his feet, to get a couple of dots and save the over."'

This coaching attitude is unwittingly damaging to self-confidence because it has the power of negative suggestion. It is rather like saying to someone, 'Don't think of ice cream.' It is then the first thing that comes into one's head. Talk of failure has the same effect, with much worse consequences. It is counter-productive. Jenner's teaching was unlikely to produce quick results amid the short-termism and conservatism of county cricket.

Some golfers having problems with confidence adopt specifically non-technical language when working on how to improve. The South African Ernie Els tried to regulate the rhythm of his swing by mouthing the word 'fish' when making his upswing, the word 'and' when it reached the top and the word 'chips' on the downswing. All that was in his mind when hitting was the phrase 'fish and chips'. It was effective and purposefully simple. Far better than thinking about technical refinements at the moment of performance.

So stressful can leg spin get that some give it up altogether. One bowler good enough to be selected for an academy run by the ECB found he was having trouble landing the ball and developed 'avoidance behaviour', says Barker. It felt easier for him to stop than persist. How sad. The leg-spinner who approached Barker and Jones is still playing occasionally, but at a more sedate level.

The programme devised for the voluntary patient was remedial, but what is the best way to teach leg spin from the start? Simply to get youngsters to give the ball a rip and enjoy themselves before refining their technique later to bring accuracy? Or concentrating from the start on getting the ball in the right place and letting the spin take care of itself? It is a debate which has exercised English coaches and top players throughout much of the past century.

There are parallels in discussions of the best way to teach children the skills they need in life. The more traditional theories demand coaching in the 'basics' such as reading and writing before moving educationally on to more expressive academic pursuits. Those on the more 'progressive' side instead recommend nurturing a sense of creativity and freedom before imposing grammatical, logical boundaries.

Leg spin requires considerable technical prowess to make it reliable and imagination to make it effective in a match situation.

Father Marriott, himself a school teacher, recognised leg-spin bowling was an 'addiction'.

Like other addictions, it came with unpleasant side-effects. The high was to bowl a good ball; the low was minor disaster. 'It is more likely that the memory will be one glimpse of the promised land amidst a stormy sea of full tosses, long hops, anguished oaths and umpires' signals,' wrote Marriott, 'but that glimpse is a vision never forgotten.'

In a schoolmasterly way Marriott decided that teaching control of line and length from the outset was the only way to protect youngsters from humiliation. 'Some people advocate urging a young bowler simply to spin the ball as hard as he can and leave control until later,' he complained. 'I am dead against any such thing: not only is "later" almost certain to be "too late", but it can lead to a pernicious habit, very difficult to cure – that of trying to spin the ball too hard *at the expense of control*, on a turning wicket or a slow one, with the inevitable tendency to bowl short in the very conditions in which it is absolutely essential to pitch the ball well up.'

Marriott's theory has logic, but leg spin is not, when it comes down to it, a very logical way for a young person to choose to bowl. Its rewards are hard to achieve.

In 1937 the Essex and England all-rounder Stan Nichols described what he called a 'counsel of perfection' offered to English leg-spinners, expected to bowl a good length, in the right direction, with deceptive flight, at varied pace and interposed with variations such as top spinners and googlies.

Don Bradman, vulnerable by his own unsurpassed standards to the best leg-spinners, acknowledged the difficulties, 'Perhaps that is why they mature rather later, on the average, than other types. Perhaps also it is the reason why they are somewhat rare in English county cricket, where the old pros, whose job includes moulding the young bowlers, are notoriously averse to bowling which may be termed erratic.'

Bradman, brought up on Australian wickets, realised the ideal type of leg spin involved wristiness combined with accuracy. He saw the virtue of a good finger spinner like Eric Hollies, who was better than a 'wild erratic flipper', but felt 'the combination of finger spin and wrist flick is the best, providing the wristy bowler has gained sufficient accuracy'.

Hollies, hurt as a young man by a Wally Hammond onslaught, felt the 'spin first, accuracy later' school of bowling was a destructive force, as it did not provide the basic technique required. This was unsurprising of a bowler renowned for his ability to cause 'toothache' with his consistency.

Hollies thought leg spin harder to teach than off spin, as one could reach proficiency at the latter with little 'natural talent'. The off break had the thumb and two fingers to control it, while the normally held leg break relied on just the third finger for control, he argued. This increased the need to instil accuracy as early as possible.

It is equally unsurprising that Australian Arthur Mailey, known as a 'millionaire' bowler because of his disdain for dot balls and maidens and a desire always to attack, took the opposite view. He felt youngsters should spin as hard as possible to give them the tools to turn the ball on the least receptive pitches Test cricket had to offer. And when Mailey played in the 1920s those on offer in his home country were very unresponsive indeed.

Hollies and Mailey represent what might loosely be termed the 'English' and 'Australian' schools of leg-spin teaching. The English was designed for pitches where turn was more easily achieved but accuracy was important because of the slow pace. The Australian way was less about containment than getting something out of the most stubborn surfaces, but which offered bounce and life when utilised properly.

There is a sort of 'third way'. Ian Peebles, who thought about the subject for years and wrote about it often in his newspaper columns, wanted a less prescriptive, more personalised approach:

> I have seen many good prospects disconcerted and eventually ruined by dogmatic orders to bowl faster or slower or spin more or less. Only the bowler himself knows what feels comfortable and right and so engenders that confidence which is essential to successful attack.

He noted that over-coaching was the greatest sin if based on misguided ideas:

> In 1929 I bowled at the opposite end to Walter Robins and have no hesitation in saying he was the most dangerous leg-break bowler in England, and maybe in the world. He bowled his spinners at a very sharp pace with a full long swing and the ball seemingly lost no pace from the manipulation of his fingers. He made no attempt to flight the ball, beyond its tendency to dip from his tremendous spin. At times he was inaccurate, a fault which would have diminished, but at all times he was highly dangerous.
>
> He made but one major mistake. He listened to the pundits who, having never bowled a 'tweaker' in their lives, insisted that he should flight the ball. His experiments in

COUNSELLORS OF PERFECTION

this direction were only partially successful, and robbed the general performance of its extraordinary snap and verve. The result was that although Walter remained a fine bowler for some years afterwards he never, to my mind, realised his full greatness nor again reached his early power of destruction.

Robins agreed with the need to keep things simple. His son Richard remembers his father telling him and his brother Charles, 'Well, anybody could open a door.' In other words, he emphasised the naturalness of applying twist to a ball, likening it to turning a door handle. It was a concise way of explaining to his boys what they must do. He advocated bowling mainly off breaks, interspersed with the odd leg break, until the shoulder was mature enough to take greater strain. The googly, more strenuous still, was not to be attempted until later.

In the 1970s the former Australian Test player Peter Philpott pushed for a re-popularising of leg spin. His advice, which he still gives to this day, is to 'bowl normally for you', in a style felt to be 'natural and comfortable'.

He agrees that the current pitches in county cricket, less damp than in the uncovered days, would allow leg spin to prosper. Philpott's real problem is with the surfaces young players learn on. They are soft and slow, encouraging medium pace and flat finger spin. Shane Warne's success inspired hopeful imitators in the 1990s and since but the conditions for their early development remain poor. Allied to a county system that is at best dubious about their merits and a lack of understanding from coaches along the way, there is little chance of success.

All the pedagogical theories had their own merits, but what would work now? English leg spin at first-class level is still more or less obsolete after decades of decline and dormancy. Without the cultural base to stimulate a more organic recovery, it is wise to look at the experience of China, whose athletes went from missing all Olympic Games from 1956 to 1980 to gaining 100 medals at Beijing 2008, 51 of them golds. The country invested many millions of pounds in creating a sporting programme to mirror its economic transformation.

It is especially strong in table tennis, gymnastics, badminton and diving, but has not known the same success in men's swimming. In 1992 China won its first Olympic women's gold in the pool. Yet male events, dominated by Americans and Australians, took 20 years longer to conquer. Finally, at London 2012, a Chinese man, Sun Yang, took the men's 400m, with Ye Shiwen winning the 400m individual medley final a few minutes later. The great powers of swimming were now facing serious competition.

How did China start creating men's champions? As it became more open to the world, the country sent its elite swimmers overseas to take advantage of the expertise available, particularly in Australia and the US. Sun spent 70 days training down under before travelling to London. 'The best benefit they get by training abroad is the one-notch-up performance,' Zhuang Yong, a sports writer for China's Xinhua news agency, explained. 'Sun and other swimmers are very strong already. What they need is a golden touch.'

Even the top performers could only reach a certain level of performance at home. Their trips abroad were similar in intent to Terry Jenner's scheme. The notable difference is how much more time the Chinese authorities were willing to allow swimmers to develop their 'golden touch'. They wanted to learn from others, not just delegate the training of champions to overseas experts. How long until other nations look to China for guidance on conquering men's swimming? Proper effort can overcome a national inferiority complex.

Being good at leg spin, like swimming, indeed involves a 'counsel of perfection'. It is hard, hard work, which taxes the mind as much as the body. Practitioners need all the help they can get.

What Now?

'It is difficult to imagine Abdul Qadir
being allowed to survive and flower
in Yorkshire.'

Mike Brearley

IN his final radio interview before dying in 1995, England and Worcestershire's Roly Jenkins recited the famous words of Lord Harris, who dominated the game's administration in the late 19th and early 20th centuries, 'Cricket. It is a moral lesson in itself, and the classroom is God's air and sunshine. Foster it, my brothers.

'Protect it from anything that will sully it, so that it will be in favour with all men.'

'What would he do in his grave,' Jenkins asked, 'if he could see what was going on today?'

But even in this barren land for leggies there are some reasons to be cheerful. During the 2013/14 Ashes series the selectors did something brave. They picked a specialist leg-spinner in a match against Australia for the first time since the 1960s.

In all that time, when England had struggled against Shane Warne, Stuart MacGill and others, Australia's batsmen, among them Allan Border, Steve Waugh, Greg Chappell, Ricky Ponting and Mark Taylor, had never faced the same challenge. While Warne took 195 wickets against England, not one proper bowler even tried to do so against Australia.

The leg-spinner England chose to make at least a partial correction to this imbalance was Scott Borthwick, a blond-haired 23-year-old from Durham. With England already 4-0 down in the five-Test series, he got the call-up. There was nothing to lose.

Borthwick came into the attack at Sydney, known as a spinners' ground, with two of Australia's best batsmen, Steve Smith and Brad Haddin, already settled. His collar turned up, he rubbed his right hand in the dirt, twirled the ball a few times from right hand to left and prepared to bowl. Haddin, in the pre-match banter, had promised the team would attack Borthwick, targeting him as the Australians do any perceived weakness.

Shane Warne watched from the commentary box, tempering leg spin-lovers' hopes with the caveat that one cannot expect accuracy from an inexperienced player.

Borthwick bowled his first ball without disaster. A few more followed and he appeared to become more confident. The legacy of Terry Jenner's coaching was evident in a strong body action and a willingness to toss the ball up. It was beginning to look okay.

Another caveat came from David Gower. 'The trouble for any leg-spinner, now and for the next 100 years,' he said, 'is that they will always be compared to the best. That's Shane Warne.' Gower was over-estimating the historical awareness of the average cricket fan. After all, who talks of S.F. Barnes in that way now, just over 100 years after he left Test cricket? But we got his point.

Nasser Hussain chipped in to remind Sky Sports viewers that, since 1970, English leg-spinners had taken 24 Test wickets at 93, while Australia's had taken 1,229 at 30.

Borthwick, a jolly soul, kept going. Then, with the third ball of his fifth over, he did it. He got a wicket. Left-hander Mitchell Johnson slogged the ball to long-on where substitute fielder Joe Root held a high catch. According to my research this was the first Ashes wicket for an English leg-spinner since Bob Barber had Graham McKenzie caught by John Snow for a duck at Old Trafford in 1968.

Borthwick was obviously a raw talent. He bowled several full tosses but managed to beat the bat when he pitched the ball correctly. In the second innings he took three wickets: opener Chris Rogers, tail-ender Ryan Harris and Haddin, the man who had promised the punishment.

His figures for the match were 4-82 off just 13 overs. It was not containing or accurate, but it got people out. In a match at the end of a long-lost series, Borthwick's was a good selection. If he could return to Durham and get some overs 'under his belt' he looked a real prospect. As the 2014 season began, he saw clearly his role and need to develop. 'In four-day cricket leg-spinners are still wicket-takers, but you try and build pressure by bowling long spells for not many runs and tie an end up, sending down five or six maidens and then get the batsman out.'

He also realised the difficulties he might face. 'I think any spinner has to accept being hit for sixes because you're inevitably going to bowl the odd bad ball. The great man Shane Warne bowled a few bad balls and he was the best leg-spinner in the word, so you've got to stay calm, bounce back and think positively.'

So how did the 2014 season go? Borthwick did very well, but not as a leg-spinner. With his all-round talent he played as Durham's number three batsman, amassing 1,187 runs at 43.96. The seamer-friendly pitches at Chester-le-Street meant others did most of the bowling. Borthwick managed just 183.2 overs in the season. He took 13 wickets at 58.61.

England did not come calling again, preferring the burgeoning part-time off spin of Moeen Ali as they lost to Sri Lanka and beat India. It was disappointing for Borthwick, but hopefully his positive attitude will mean he can once again come into consideration as much for his bowling as his batting. 'He needs to get plenty of overs in,' argues Ian Salisbury. 'Otherwise there's no way he can progress to being the bowler he can and should be.'

Elsewhere, Sussex leg-spinner Will Beer managed one first-class match in 2014, taking 0-76, being used mainly as a one-day bowler. Max Waller of Somerset did not play a County Championship match.

A sadder fate awaited Tom Craddock, who was laid off by Essex after England left-arm spinner Monty Panesar was brought in from Sussex following his sacking for urinating on a nightclub bouncer on Brighton seafront. Craddock departed the first-class game with a bowling average of 30.51. He was 25 years old, almost a decade younger than Australia's Clarrie Grimmett had been when he made his Test debut.

Craddock made headlines in 2013, taking five wickets for Essex against England at Chelmsford in a special pre-Ashes warm-up. His victims were Kevin Pietersen, Ian Bell, Matt Prior, Graeme Swann and Steven Finn. 'An unbelievable achievement,' he declared at the time. 'I'm chuffed to bits with it.' Asked, inevitably, if he would be the next Shane Warne, he smiled and replied, 'We'll see about that one. I'll just take it one step at a time. I'll just keep trying to take wickets and see where we go from there.'

Robin Hobbs, who made his way with Essex half a century before, is unhappy at the signing of Panesar. 'Craddock bowled bloody well against England,' he says. 'He was going to play the last seven county games of the season and his mother got terminally ill. He had to go back to Yorkshire, where he's from. That's why we've now signed Panesar, much to everybody's absolute disgust. Where does that put Craddock? He's now just going to drift out of the game.'

To cap Craddock's disappointment, the warm-up match against England does not even have first-class status in the records. It lost this after two Essex players were injured and had to be replaced.

One leg-spinner who does appear to be on the rise again is Yorkshire's Adil Rashid. Hobbs has always rated the Bradford-born all-rounder, who played five one-dayers and five T20 matches for England in 2009 and 2010. 'I admire Rashid,' he says. 'I think he's a bloody good cricketer. I think England should look at him again. His leg-break bowling went down the hill a little bit but it's improved again. I'm not sure England would go back to him. If you don't fit into a category and tick all the boxes, your card's marked, I'm sure.'

Rashid, who began bowling leg spin at the age of nine, has an unorthodox action. He is more open-chested than prescribed under the Terry Jenner system. In fact Salisbury thinks he was left 'confused' by his time in Adelaide under Jenner's tutelage and that his natural talent needs to be left to flourish.

In 2009 Graeme Swann predicted great things for him, albeit demonstrating a lack of historical knowledge of leg spin. 'Adil is a long way down the line with leg spin at 20,' he said. 'He is probably better than anyone there has ever been bar one Australian fella. But he will admit he is nowhere near the finished article – he needs to develop, learn, and play more cricket basically. It is exciting for England just how good he is at 20. He could be exceptional at 25 and a world-beater by 30. Hopefully he will be.'

But his Yorkshire captain at the time, Anthony McGrath, sounded a note of caution when he was picked to tour with England in the West Indies. 'We have got to learn from what has gone before with the likes of Chris Schofield, who played a couple of matches and that was it. I am not saying that Adil can't perform now at that level but, as a young player, you will get dips in form.

'As a club, and as a national team with all their people around, we have all got to support him in those low times to make sure that he is sustainable in the next ten to 15 years.'

The number of revolutions per minute achieved by England's spinners was measured in 2010 using TrackMan, a device adapted from golf, which involved placing a small camera behind the bowler's arm. Rashid topped the list with 2,312. Unfortunately he did not have a good time on the South Africa tour of 2009/10. When he returned to England, it was said he had been told to speed up his action. His figures declined.

Mark Lawson, by then laid off by Yorkshire, was moved to tell the *Daily Express* that Rashid was being under-used by the county. 'The main problem is nothing to do with pitches or conditions; it's that we still have a want for immediate success,' he said. 'As a leg-spin bowler even up to the age of 28 or 29 you're still going to have good years and bad years… I spent two seasons as a 12th man, not playing cricket. The most important thing for any leg-spinner is to bowl a lot of overs but you need support.'

By the beginning of 2013 Rashid was beginning to feel frustrated at Yorkshire. His career was not progressing as he wanted, let alone as Swann had predicted. He was strongly critical of captain Andrew Gale when he spoke to the *Independent*. 'I've been playing here seven years and I want to stay,' he said. 'But I have a career and I can't waste another year.' Rashid complained that he had not had adequate backing. 'If I don't feel as though I've been treated well, I'll go,' he added. 'It's hard to come straight on and hit your length and line with every delivery if you're hardly bowling and the coaches and people around you don't give you the backing.' Rashid argued Gale was only giving him brief spells.

He appeared to be fulfilling the prediction made by former England captain Mike Brearley in 1985, three years before Rashid was born. 'Leg spin, with its flourish and strut, its long-hops and its patches of brilliance, is anathema to the Yorkshire mentality. It is difficult to imagine Abdul Qadir being allowed to survive and flower in Yorkshire; and if the next small, flexible-jointed Qadir happens to be born in Bradford, his best chance would be to move south (if not also east) at an early age.'

But Rashid made his peace with Gale and Yorkshire. He had a mediocre 2013, but the next season once again demonstrated his talent. In a Yorkshire side that stormed to the County Championship with a dominance not seen since the 1960s, he took 49 wickets at 24.81. He also scored 577 runs at 36.06. He was an all-round prospect once more, not a talented county player who had fizzled out early. He was still, after all, only 26. Rashid was picked for the short England tour to the West Indies. The chance of a leg-spinner taking part in the 2015 Ashes was not yet dead.

As for the longer term, the England and Wales Cricket Board continues its search for high-quality slow bowlers. It is no longer relying on foreign expertise like that Terry Jenner once provided. In 2012 it appointed former England off-spinner Peter Such as national head spin-bowling coach. The role includes developing skills at county level. He oversees a programme placing a specialist spin-bowling coach with every county and first-class university side.

Such has worked with Borthwick and Simon Kerrigan, the Lancashire left-armer who had a difficult debut in the final match of the 2013 Ashes, when he had trouble finding his length and was smashed about. He predicted both would add to their single cap:

> It's tough stepping into Test cricket, but as long as people learn from the experience it can only be a good thing.
>
> There are some quality spin bowlers in the pipeline. It is a matter of whether we can get them through into first-team cricket and then onwards.
>
> The game is different from years ago when you would have two spin bowlers in any team, usually an experienced one and a younger one learning the trade. That was a great learning environment and more overs of spin were bowled.
>
> Now spin bowlers tend to be lone practitioners and, as a consequence, less spin bowling is being seen at senior level.

Swann, the off-spinner who took more than 200 Test wickets before retiring midway through the 2013/14 Ashes, has done some mentoring work. He and Such may not have bowled leg spin but they understand what it takes to prosper as a slow bowler at the highest level. The few leg-spinners in the English first-class game and their would-be successors need all the assistance they can get.

The recent age of truly sensational Test match spinners – Shane Warne, Muttiah Muralitharan and Anil Kumble at the peak – has ended. Yet that is not to say we live in unexciting times. As well as traditional styles, there has been a growth in the number of 'mystery' bowlers on the international scene. Ajantha Mendis of Sri Lanka and Sunil Narine of the West Indies are among those flummoxing batsmen with their oddities. The carrom ball, flicked between the thumb and a bent middle finger, is becoming more prevalent. The doosra is still in use, although, as in the case of Pakistan's Saeed Ajmal, it can cause problems to an off-spinner's action, potentially rendering it illegal with a requirement to bend the arm too far.

And, it appears, there is scope for an almost googly-like degree of innovation among traditional leg-spinners, without the need for any semblance of illegality. Sports scientists Aaron Beach, René Ferdinands and Peter Sinclair of Sydney University have seemingly discovered a new way to exploit the Magnus effect, the sideways movement through the air created by the disruption of air flow caused by a spinning ball. Remember, the Magnus effect is what allowed the 'Barnes ball' of the early 20th century and '*that* ball' bowled by Warne at Old Trafford in 1993 to happen.

Beach, Ferdinands and Sinclair looked at the movement through the air of different types of spinners. They found that, although leg-spinners have historically been thought to have the ability to swerve the ball in to the right-handed batsman before pitching, two of those they studied had managed the opposite – that is, swerve away – with ostensibly the same action. 'This ability may be the exclusive domain of leg-spinners alone,' they said. 'It may even be feasible to train leg-spin bowlers to spin balls in the same direction… giving them the ability to swerve a ball to the left and right, even though it has the same direction of spin.'

Without any discernible variation, the ball could swerve in *or* out before hitting the pitch and turning away. It would take some batsman to deal with that. How one can teach this level of controllable subtlety is baffling, but someone might do it.

Before Bosanquet came along, mainstream cricketing opinion had not conceptualised the googly. A fast leg break was mere fantasy before Barnes. If anyone achieves what Beach, Ferdinands and Sinclair suggest, it will make the technical requirements of top-class leg spin even harder and the rewards potentially larger. That is what sporting evolution is all about.

We led the world at the start of the last century but lost touch with our own genius. If English cricket can get the basics back in place and start fostering a new generation of first-class and then Test leg-spinners, who knows what might happen?

Manifesto

It is not going to be easy reversing decades of neglect. But here are six ideas which might help.

1) Bring back twisti-twosti

It sounds like a quaint pastime which should be consigned to the billiards rooms of Victorian and Edwardian country houses, but this simple game helped Bernard Bosanquet to develop the most outrageous challenge to cricket's established order when he popularised the googly in the early 1900s. The table-top game, involving contortions of the wrist, encourages familiarity with spinning a ball and the deception of opponents through guile. These are skills lacking in the English game. Exposure to them as youngsters can do nothing but good. All the game requires is a tennis ball, two or four people and a table. It does not have to be a snooker table. Anything covered in felt will do. Cricket clubs should encourage twisti-twosti during the winter. The ECB could even sell sets.

2) Talk to the captains

The biggest problem after the rise of Shane Warne and the explosion of would-be leg-spinners in England keen to emulate him was not a lack of supply but a lack of genuine demand. The ECB wanted more leggies. More people wanted to be leggies. But the counties showed little appetite for so high-risk and high-investment a form of bowling. All the pupils of Terry Jenner who have made it to first-class level have experienced mistrust by their leaders. The ECB should invite someone like Warne or Stuart MacGill to talk to county captains, extolling the virtues of leg spin, its attacking potential and how to handle it effectively. This would result in more trust and better fields. Captains at club and age-group level would also benefit and be inspired by Warne and others' charisma. The demand would then be genuine, rather than just lip service to a centralised scheme.

3)   Celebrate its history

The national inferiority complex over leg spin has resulted in another broken link – between the present and the more glorious past. Players know little of the exploits of Tich Freeman, S.F. Barnes or Bernard Bosanquet. Learning about past masters would show players there was a time when Englishmen, not Indians, Pakistanis, Sri Lankans and Australians, were the innovators. Someone like David Frith, Robin Hobbs or Amol Rajan, with their extensive knowledge of the game's history and the ability to impart it in an engaging way, could serve as a sort of ambassador between eras. It would show leg spin in England is not a charity case, but a viable and exciting career.

4)   Look at balls and pitches

English leg-spinners who have gone on to play in Australia frequently cite the Kookaburra ball as being easier to grip and land properly than the Dukes variety used at home. This should be studied in a scientific way. If it is found to be true, the ECB might consider adopting the other type in first-class games. ECB pitch adviser Chris Wood's efforts to prolong bounce even in deteriorating surfaces should be studied too. First-class pitches in England are not really the problem, but every little helps. Perhaps his findings should be taken into account when preparing pitches to be used by children and teenagers, which do not encourage leg spin, such is their flat, damp nature.

5) Bring back the lost ones

Leg-spinners are said to mature late. That is why it is so sad
that the likes of Michael Munday and Mark Lawson were out
of contract well before the age of 30. They had barely reached
leg-spinning adolescence. Like Ian Salisbury in the latter stages
of his career, they have since gained a mature understanding
of what is needed by spending time out of the game. Lawson
is a respected coach, Munday a highly successful league player
with a formidable brain. They could be valuable additions to
county staffs, perhaps on a part-time basis. They would freshen
up County Championship cricket.

6) Bring back amateurism

I do not mean it is time to recreate the snobbish distinction
between gentlemen and players. Rather, English cricket should
try to recapture the spirit of adventure rarely seen in the last 50
or 60 years. For every Botham performance or Gower innings
there have been weeks of dour, attritional cricket. Leg spin, as
Scott Borthwick demonstrated during his spirited Test debut
in 2013/14, enlivens the game. Taking risks, rather than simply
gaining massive leads and then wearing down batting sides with
seam and off spin/left-arm spin, would bring crowds back in. Leg-
spinners raise run rates and create chances. With the popularity
of Test cricket declining in most parts of the world and first-class
cricket watched by tiny crowds, the game needs leg spin more
than ever, even in England.

Pessimism is the natural response to the situation in which leg
spin in England still finds itself. But understanding how we have
got to this low ebb – better than the nadir of the 1980s, but not
much – is necessary to try to rise from it.

   It is not only in England that there is a problem, but it is more
established than in most Test-playing countries. Australia's Peter
Philpott says the system there is also letting would-be leggies
down badly now, with top players having less contact with others

through Grade and even first-class cricket, such are modern itineraries, and a growing emphasis on T20. Ian Chappell has recently bemoaned a lack of leg spin at state level. For the game's sake, it should not be allowed to perish there as in England.

'It's often said you can't shape your future unless you remember your past,' says Chappell.

Philpott offers these words of advice. 'Spin, spin and be merry.' We should give both ideas a try.

Dramatis Personae

Allan Gibson Steel
England, Lancashire, Cambridge University
Born: 24 September 1858, Liverpool
Died: 15 June 1914, Hyde Park, London
Tests: 29 wickets at 20.86
First-class: 789 wickets at 14.78

Coming from a cricket-obsessed family, Steel was a teenage prodigy, rated by his teachers at Marlborough College as one of the best spinners in the country. He went to Cambridge University and, playing there and for Lancashire, managed 164 wickets in his first season in first-class cricket, using a mixture of leg breaks and off breaks. His figures gradually declined over the next few years, but he remained an excellent all-round player for county and country, scoring eight first-class centuries, two of them in Tests. He is regarded as England's first out-and-out international leg-spinner. Steel had a long career in the law. He became recorder of Oldham, having gained a reputation as one of the best barristers in England. He also served as an England Test selector.

Walter Mead
England, Essex
Born: 1 April 1868, Clapton, London
Died: 18 March 1954, Ongar, Essex
Tests: 1 wicket at 91.00
First-class: 1,916 wickets at 18.99

A very reliable bowler, pushing the ball down at near medium pace, Mead was not a big spinner of the ball. However, he is credited with bowling the googly, at least occasionally, before Bernard Bosanquet made it famous. He also bowled the off break. His one Test, against Australia at Lord's in 1899, was not a success. At county level he twice took 17 wickets in a match.

Sydney Francis Barnes
England, Lancashire, Warwickshire, Staffordshire, Wales
Born: 19 April 1873, Smethwick, Staffordshire
Died: 26 December 1967, Chadsmoor, Staffordshire
Tests: 189 wickets at 16.43
First-class: 719 wickets at 17.09

To this day Barnes is rated by many as the finest bowler to have played the game. He bowled at about 70mph but was still able to spin the ball either way using his exceptionally strong fingers. Taken on tour with England in 1902/03 on a hunch after captain Archie MacLaren saw potential in his bowling, he did well initially but gained a reputation for grumpiness and being injury-prone. He eventually became a regular England player, despite having rejected the first-class county game in favour of a better-remunerated life in league and Minor Counties cricket. In 1911/12 he broke the record for the number of wickets taken by an Englishman in an Ashes series. Barnes took a still-record 49 wickets in his final Test series, against South Africa in 1913/14. His fast leg break, nicknamed the 'Barnes ball', has never been bettered. His Test career was ended by the First World War, but Barnes kept playing into his sixties, even being asked in the early 1920s, when almost 50, whether he wanted to tour with England again. In all forms of cricket, he is said to have taken 6,220 wickets at 8.33.

Joseph Vine
England, Sussex, London County
Born: 15 May 1875, Willingdon, East Sussex
Died: 25 April 1946, Hove, East Sussex
Tests: Did not bowl
First-class: 685 wickets at 28.51

A talented batsman, Vine, a professional, was ordered by amateur opening partner C.B. Fry to rein in his attacking instincts to ensure he was not overshadowed. He did not bowl during his two Tests but at county level he was an all-rounder. Vine delivered his leg breaks at a pace rarely seen until Sydney Barnes came along, requiring the field placing of a back-stop.

Leonard Charles Braund

England, Somerset, London County
Born: 18 October 1875, Clewer, Berkshire
Died: 23 December 1955, Putney, London
Tests: 47 wickets at 38.51
First-class: 1,114 wickets at 27.27

Braund is often overlooked, having played in an era dominated by the googly antics of Bernard Bosanquet and the brilliance of Sydney Barnes, but he was a highly accomplished all-round player who gave much to the game. He moved from Surrey to Somerset, where he became a crowd favourite with his big personality and determination to win, always tempered by a sense of humour. Braund played for Somerset until 1920, hitting 25 hundreds to go with his wickets. He was also one of the best slip fielders of his era. Braund became a respected umpire and continued to watch first-class matches after he had both legs amputated during the 1940s.

Charles Lucas Townsend

England, Gloucestershire, London County
Born: 7 November 1876, Clifton, Bristol
Died: 17 October 1958, Stockton-on-Tees
Tests: Three wickets at 25.00
First-class: 725 wickets at 23.11

Townsend, a lawyer like A.G. Steel, enjoyed an early flourish as a big-spinning, wicket-taking bowler. He was also a useful batsman, but his career as a lawyer meant he had little time for cricket after his mid-twenties.

Bernard James Tindal Bosanquet

England, Middlesex, Oxford University
Born: 13 October 1877, Enfield, Middlesex
Died: 12 October 1936, Ewhurst, Surrey
Tests: 25 wickets at 24.16
First-class: 629 wickets at 23.80

Although probably not the originator of the googly, the leg-spinner's ball which turns into the right-handed batsman with a barely discernible change in action, Bosanquet was undoubtedly its great populariser. Eton and Oxford-educated and of Huguenot descent, he was an experimental character who found the grind of fast bowling tedious and so changed his style with sensational results. Bosanquet's googly was decisive in England regaining the Ashes in 1903/04, although really his was a bit-part in the context of the series as a whole, with Yorkshire left-armer Wilfred Rhodes deserving the greatest plaudits. Bosanquet's methods were emulated with more skill by bowlers in South Africa and Australia, and later in India, Sri Lanka and Pakistan. He maintained a humorous defensiveness when discussing the googly, branding it merely 'immoral' when asked whether it should be legal. Bosanquet's son Reginald was an ITN newsreader during the 1960s and 1970s.

Alfred Percy Freeman
England, Kent
Born: 17 May 1888, Lewisham, London
Died: 28 January 1965, Bearsted, Kent
Tests: 66 wickets at 25.86
First-class: 3,776 wickets at 18.42

He was known universally as 'Tich' because of his diminutive stature, during an era when nicknames seldom verged beyond the banal. Freeman's career, interrupted by the First World War, took a while to get going but, for several years during the late 1920s and 1930s, his wicket-taking feats were unparalleled. In 1928 he took 304 first-class wickets, a record unlikely to be beaten. Strangely, he was not picked to play in any Tests after 1929. He never faced Australia in England, even when Don Bradman was breaking international scoring records in 1930. There was a perception that Freeman was taking too many easy wickets for Kent and that this would not translate into the highest form of the game. Lesser bowlers were picked at his expense. It was England's loss and Kent's gain. Freeman, a quiet man of character and stamina, was sacked by Kent in 1936 but continued to organise charity matches into old age.

Thomas Leonard Richmond
England, Nottinghamshire
Born: 23 June 1890, Radcliffe-on-Trent, Nottinghamshire
Died: 29 December 1957, Saxondale, Nottinghamshire
Tests: Two wickets at 43.00
First-class: 1,176 wickets at 21.22

Not as small as Freeman, Richmond was given the same nickname – 'Tich' – as his extraordinary contemporary. For several years the two were considered the best leg break/googly bowlers in England. But whereas Freeman improved, Richmond's powers waned. Most blamed his expanding waistline.

John William Hearne
England, Middlesex
Born: 11 February 1891, Uxbridge, Middlesex
Died: 14 September 1965, Hillingdon, Middlesex
Tests: 30 wickets at 48.73
First-class: 1,839 wickets at 24.42

A modest, charming all-rounder whose career lasted from 1909 to 1936, Jack Hearne scored 96 hundreds to go with his wickets. He bowled pacey leg breaks and googlies and helped Middlesex win the County Championship in 1921. His Test bowling average was ordinary, but his first-class career was excellent.

Percy George Herbert Fender
England, Surrey, Sussex
Born: 22 August 1892, Balham, London
Died: 15 June 1985, Exeter, Devon
Tests: 29 wickets at 40.86
First-class: 1,894 wickets at 25.05

One of the true characters of first-class cricket, Fender, a tall man with a Groucho Marx-esque moustache and a liking for extremely long jumpers, dominated the Oval during the 1920s. Recognised as a superb captain, talented slip fielder and ultra-attacking batsman, he never made quite the same mark in Test matches. His bowling varied. Usually he bowled quicker-than-average leg spin, but he would try his hand at any type if it meant getting Surrey to a win. Fender went on to a long career as a wine dealer.

Charles Stowell Marriott
England, Kent, Lancashire, Cambridge University
Born: 14 September 1895, Heaton Moor, Lancashire
Died: 13 October 1966, Dollis Hill, Middlesex
Tests: 11 wickets at 8.72
First-class: 711 wickets at 20.11

To consider Marriott's career is to return to an era when even top sportsmen did not regard their performances on the pitch to be of paramount importance in life. Raised mainly in Ireland, Cambridge-educated Marriott played for Lancashire briefly before joining Kent, where he performed during holidays from teaching at Dulwich College. A tall, lean man, he had a distinctive whippy action, flinging the ball forward from a starting point behind his back. His single Test match, against West Indies in 1933, was one of the greatest debuts in internationals. His average of 8.72 stands as the lowest in the history of Tests among those who have taken ten or more wickets. Usually in Tich Freeman's shadow (metaphorically) for Kent, he later continued to teach leg spin, writing a book on the subject which was published after his death.

Richard Knowles Tyldesley
England, Lancashire
Born: 11 March 1897, Westhoughton, Lancashire
Died: 17 September 1943, Bolton, Lancashire
Tests: 19 wickets at 32.57
First-class: 1,509 wickets at 17.21

Part of a famous Lancashire cricketing family, Tyldesley cut a Falstaffian figure – overweight and jolly. He eschewed the googly in favour of the top spinner. In fact, he did not get much sideways movement with the ball either way, but was relentlessly accurate. On helpful pitches he could be deadly. He made his Test debut on the 1924/25 Ashes series in Australia, where the hard, unresponsive surfaces did not help him.

Greville Thomas Scott Stevens
England, Middlesex, Oxford University
Born: 7 January 1901, Hampstead, London
Died: 19 September 1970, Islington, London
Tests: 20 wickets at 32.40
First-class: 684 wickets at 26.84

With his matinée idol good looks, Stevens was one of the glamour players of the 1920s and 1930s. He first attracted attention by scoring 466 runs in a house match at University College School in 1919, being selected for the Gentlemen against the Players that year. His bowling tailed off towards the end of his career and he missed many matches because of his business commitments.

Thomas Bignall Mitchell
England, Derbyshire
Born: 4 September 1902, Creswell, Derbyshire
Died: 27 January 1996, Doncaster, Yorkshire
Tests: 8 wickets at 62.25
First-class: 1,483 wickets at 20.59

Mitchell, a miner, was discovered during the General Strike of 1926, when Derbyshire captain Guy Jackson spotted him during a match organised to rebuild industrial relations. He started playing for the county, his strong body action allowing him to get plenty of spin. Mitchell was a noted comedian. With this came a tendency not to take himself as seriously as some thought he should. Mitchell made his England debut in the notorious 1932/33 Bodyline series and never became established, having a particularly bad match at Lord's in 1935. He refused the terms offered by Derbyshire after the Second World War, returning to work in the pit. He lived until the age of 93.

James Morton Sims
England, Middlesex
Born: 13 May 1903, Leyton, Essex
Died: 27 April 1973, Canterbury, Kent
Tests: 11 wickets at 43.63
First-class: 1,581 wickets at 24.92

A well-loved Middlesex stalwart from the late 1920s to the early 1950s, Sims bowled a particularly quick leg break and googly, which he charmingly nicknamed the 'wozzler'. He also made almost 9,000 first-class runs and was known for his sportsmanship and good humour. He never became a regular in Test cricket, two of his matches being played on the heart-breaking Australian pitches of 1936/37. He later worked as Middlesex's scorer.

Ian Alexander Ross Peebles
England, Middlesex, Oxford University
Born: 20 January 1908, Aberdeen
Died: 27 February 1980, Speen, Buckinghamshire
Tests: 45 wickets at 30.91
First-class: 923 wickets at 21.38

Peebles was long regarded by devotees of leg spin as the one that got away. In his youth he showed promise of becoming the next Sydney Barnes but, because of injuries, technical problems and the pressure he felt under, this never materialised. Still, for a couple of years Peebles was undoubtedly one of the best leg-spinners in the world. His finest moment came at Old Trafford in 1930, where he made Don Bradman look foolish for a few overs. A genial man and protégé of South African Aubrey Faulkner, Peebles was the first Scotsman to play for England. He maintained a connection with cricket throughout his life as a journalist, while running a wine business.

Thomas Peter Bromley Smith
England, Essex
Born: 30 October 1908, Ipswich
Died: 4 August 1967, Hyères, France
Tests: 3 wickets at 106.33
First-class: 1,697 wickets at 26.55

Peter Smith is best known for being the victim of a hoax in 1933. He turned up to play for England at the Oval despite not actually having been picked. It was another 13 years until he made it to Tests, having a brief and unsuccessful career. However, his first-class career with Essex was long and productive. He worked as a film extra.

Frederick Richard Brown
England, Surrey, Northamptonshire, Cambridge University
Born: 16 December 1910, Lima, Peru
Died: 24 July 1991, Ramsbury, Wiltshire
Tests: 45 wickets at 31.06
First-class: 1,221 wickets at 26.21

Best remembered for his stoical leadership of the England Ashes team of 1950/51, who lost four-nil, Brown was as tough as they came. A slow-medium leg-spinner and quick-scoring batsman, he was very much in the amateur mould. He could be a martinet as a leader, but learned his skills under Percy Fender at Surrey and would never ask his men to do anything he would not. After the Second World War he moved to Northamptonshire. His greatest test, though, came during it. He was captured by the Germans at Tobruk in 1942 and remained a prisoner of war until 1945, losing more than four stones in weight. He made a comeback to first-class cricket in 1948, returning to England colours, having been on an MCC tour as early as the 1932/33 Bodyline series.

Johnny Lawrence
Somerset
Born: 29 March 1911, Leeds
Died: 10 December 1988, Tadcaster, Yorkshire
First-class: 798 wickets at 24.97

Turned down by Yorkshire, Johnny Lawrence was a reliable spinner for Somerset during the immediate post-war years. He returned to his home county and is best known as the mentor of Yorkshire and England batsman Geoffrey Boycott.

William Eric Hollies
England, Warwickshire
Born: 5 June 1912, Old Hill, Staffordshire
Died: 16 April 1981, Chinley, Derbyshire
Tests: 44 wickets at 30.27
First-class: 2,323 wickets at 20.94

Eric Hollies – he was known by his middle name – will always be associated with the dismissal of Don Bradman for a duck in his final Test innings at the Oval in 1948. But Hollies had a long and distinguished career for Warwickshire, having been able to bowl leg breaks and googlies since early boyhood. He did not look for huge turn, using his fingers rather than his wrist to spin the ball, but his style provided the accuracy more often seen among off-spinners. Hollies studied hard to become a professional cricketer, taking bodybuilding classes before the Second World War to increase his stamina. His relationship with the England team was often fraught, not being picked between 1935 and 1947 after he injured himself in a clash with a team-mate. Whether it was horseplay or an accident, the selectors were not impressed. Possibly as a result of not being consistently picked, Hollies was initially reluctant to play at the Oval in 1948. His love of Warwickshire and cricket in general never dimmed and he continued to pick up wickets in vast numbers in the Birmingham League after he quit the first-class game.

Douglas Vivian Parson Wright
England, Kent
Born: 21 August 1914, Sidcup, Kent
Died: 13 November 1998, Canterbury, Kent
Tests: 108 wickets at 39.11
First-class: 2,056 wickets at 23.98

For more than 20 years Wright perplexed English cricket and himself. Why was it that a bowler at one moment capable of bowling so many unplayable deliveries could the next be rendered impotent by inaccuracy and lack of confidence? Wright, like Peebles a protégé of Aubrey Faulkner, bowled at well above the average pace for a spinner. If not quite as quick as Barnes he was definitely not much slower than medium pace. He had leg breaks and googlies at his disposal. It is no coincidence that this unassuming Kent player holds the record for the most first-class hat-tricks with seven. His 13-step run-up, likened to a man leaping about to avoid puddles, might explain his erratic tendencies. Yet he remains England's most successful out-and-out leg-spinner, in terms of Test wickets taken.

Leonard Litton Wilkinson
England, Lancashire
Born: 5 November 1916, Northwich, Cheshire
Died: 3 September 2002, Barrow-in-Furness, Lancashire
Tests: 7 wickets at 38.71
First-class: 282 wickets at 25.25

Wilkinson played in three Tests against South Africa after a prolific burst for Lancashire in 1938, aged 21. He faded from the scene shortly after the Second World War.

Roland Oliver Jenkins
England, Worcestershire
Born: 24 November 1918, Worcester
Died: 22 July 1995, Worcester
Tests: 32 wickets at 34.31
First-class: 1,309 wickets at 23.64

Rarely can a man have loved his art as much as Jenkins. This son of Worcester, born, shaped, made aware on the city's playing fields, was obsessed with getting things right. Often seen at the nets by 7am, he would bowl away for hours, honing his 'mechanics'. He got big turn but never aspired to the same accuracy as Eric Hollies, a lifelong friend. Jenkins had a droll sense of humour, which sometimes got him into trouble. He became a cult figure among Worcestershire supporters and was free with his advice for players who followed him.

Edric Leadbeater
England, Yorkshire, Warwickshire
Born: 15 August 1927, Huddersfield
Died: 17 April 2011, Huddersfield
Tests: Two wickets at 109.00
First-class: 289 wickets at 27.49

'Eddie' Leadbeater was a decent leg-spinner in an age when his county, Yorkshire, was awash with spinning talent, most notably Bob Appleyard, Johnny Wardle and Ray Illingworth. He was surprisingly called up for two Tests against India in 1951/52 but did not prosper. Never awarded a Yorkshire cap, he played for a while for Warwickshire before giving up cricket for life as a travelling salesman.

William Thomas Greensmith
Essex
Born: 16 August 1930, Middlesbrough
First-class: 733 wickets at 28.93

In the years after the Second World War Greensmith became the main leg-spinner for Essex, taking over from England man Peter Smith and eventually making way for another Test bowler in Robin Hobbs. He was known to sport a 'Teddy boy' haircut.

Thomas Greenhough
England, Lancashire
Born: 9 November 1931, Rochdale, Lancashire
Died: 15 September 2009, Rochdale, Lancashire
Tests: 16 wickets at 22.31
First-class: 751 wickets at 22.37

It nearly ended so very early for Greenhough. Soon after having been taken on by Lancashire, aged 18, he was lucky to escape with his life when he fell 40 feet down a shaft in a cotton mill where he was working. He broke both his ankles but made his way back, entering first-class cricket in 1951. Greenhough, who had a longish approach to the wicket and got a good amount of work on the ball, picked up wickets steadily, if unspectacularly, over the next few seasons, earning a call-up in 1959 and taking five wickets in an innings against India at Lord's, making him the last English leg-spinner to achieve this feat in a Test match. But he experienced problems with his follow-through and missed the next couple of matches. Greenhough played four Tests, finally retiring from the professional game in 1966. His Test figures suggest he deserved a more prolonged chance.

Robert William Barber
England, Lancashire, Warwickshire, Cambridge University
Born: 26 September 1935, Withington, Manchester
Tests: 42 wickets at 43.00
First-class: 549 wickets at 29.46

Apart from Doug Wright, Barber is the most prolific Test wicket-taker since the Second World War among England's leg-spinners. Lasting as an England player for most of the 1960s, he gave the ball a rip. Barber also scored 1,495 Test and 17,631 first-class runs. He moved from Lancashire to Warwickshire and gradually moved from being a bowling all-rounder to an entertaining left-handed batsman of high class and more occasional bowler. Barber later made a fortune from toiletry products and now lives in Switzerland.

Robin Nicholas Stuart Hobbs
England, Essex, Glamorgan
Born: 8 May 1942, Chippenham, Wiltshire
Tests: 12 wickets at 40.08
First-class: 1,099 wickets at 27.09

From a young age Hobbs became obsessed with spinning a ball. He practised for hours in his back garden and in the parks of his home town of Dagenham. Wanted by Kent, he chose Essex instead. Not a huge turner of the ball, he was, like Eric Hollies, very accurate. Hobbs played most of his Tests against India and Pakistan, who cope with the turning ball better than most. He was not helped by having finger spinners Derek Underwood and Ray Illingworth around at the same time. Hobbs came out of retirement to captain Glamorgan but, by the time he quit for a second time in the early 1980s, he was the only English leg-spinner of any note left. He was also the last to take 1,000 first-class wickets. Hobbs, a friendly man and kindly coach, continues to help would-be leggies and to be involved with his beloved Essex.

Amritt Harrichand Latchman
Middlesex, Nottinghamshire
Born: 26 July 1943, Kingston, Jamaica
First-class wickets: 487 at 27.90

'Harry' Latchman, brought up in west London, cut an anachronistic figure in county cricket from the mid-1960s until the mid-1970s. Small of build, he tossed the ball up in a way followers of Tich Freeman would have appreciated decades earlier. He coached at Merchant Taylors' School, in Middlesex, after retiring.

Alan Terry Castell
Hampshire
Born: 6 August 1943, Oxford
First-class wickets: 229 at 30.97

Castell started off as a leg-spinner but became a medium-pacer, reasoning that this would give him a more solid career.

Warwick Nigel Tidy
Warwickshire
Born: 10 February 1953, Birmingham
First-class wickets: 81 at 34.25

Tidy, named after early 20th century author Warwick Deeping, rather than the great Australian all-rounder Warwick Armstrong, made his debut for Warwickshire at the age of 17. He had a good first year but faded from the scene after being advised to slow down his bowling. Tidy went on to a successful career in banking and finance and now runs his own gardening business in Devon. An enthusiastic character, he continues to help out aspiring leg-spinners.

Andrew Russell Clarke
Sussex
Born: 23 December 1961, Patcham, Sussex
First-class: 53 wickets at 35.32

Clarke went from club cricket to the first-class scene in 1988 when Sussex decided that leg spin might be a useful attacking weapon, such was its obscurity. He did not disappoint, picking up 44 wickets in his first season and prospering in one-day matches. His chances soon dwindled as Sussex brought in the younger Ian Salisbury, who gave the ball more spin. He left in 1990 and had a long career with Minor Counties teams.

Ian David Kenneth Salisbury
England, Sussex, Surrey, Warwickshire
Born: 21 January 1970, Northampton
Tests: 20 wickets at 76.95
First-class: 884 wickets at 32.65

Salisbury, who came on the scene in the late 1980s, was soon seen as a young leg-spinner with genuine international potential. Largely self-taught, he moved from Northampton to Hove, via the Lord's ground staff. By 1992, aged 22, he was in the Test side. An encouraging debut saw him take five wickets, his first being Javed Miandad, and great things were forecast. It was downhill after that for England, but Salisbury continued to be an effective attacking bowler in county cricket. After retiring, Salisbury coached Surrey. He now assists with England's youth teams.

Christopher Paul Schofield
England, Lancashire, Surrey
Born: 6 October 1978, Rochdale, Greater Manchester
Tests: No wickets
First-class: 237 wickets at 36.40

Picked to play for England aged just 21, Schofield never fulfilled his potential in the first-class game, although some blame should be attached to those who pushed him too far too early. Dropped after two Tests, he fell out with Lancashire and spent a year playing Minor Counties cricket and doing odd jobs to make a living, before Surrey offered him another chance. He excelled in T20 cricket, earning a call-up to the England team in this format of the game. Thereafter his performances tailed off and he was released by Surrey in 2011. He coaches and still plays for the Lashings side.

Matthew Thomas Gitsham
Gloucestershire
Born: 1 February 1982, Truro, Cornwall
First-class: 3 wickets at 90.33

Gitsham had a brief first-class career, having fallen out of love with the game after spending time in Australia under Terry Jenner's tutelage. But after university Gitsham decided to give cricket another try and worked for months to get his bowling to county standard. He runs a carpet and upholstery-cleaning business in Bristol.

Michael Kenneth Munday
Somerset, Oxford University
Born: 22 October 1984, Nottingham
First-class: 86 wickets at 29.46

Munday is a gifted leg-spinner. Terry Jenner, with whom he stayed in Australia, thought his wrist action was rivalled only by Shane Warne among those he had taught. Yet Munday, who has a first-class degree from Oxford University, did not always agree with Jenner's methods, arguing they were too dogmatic. Jenner, in return, thought Cornish-raised Munday had departed from the course most likely to bring him success. Somerset released Munday aged 25. He plays club cricket for Horsham, in Sussex, and works for an insurance company.

Mark Anthony Kenneth Lawson
Yorkshire, Middlesex, Derbyshire, Kent
Born: 24 October 1985, Leeds
First-class: 52 wickets at 43.82

If England waited many years for a decent leg-spinner to come along, Yorkshire was one of the more barren areas. So it excited the romantics and traditionalists when the White Rose county started using not one but two in the first team. Bowling in tandem with Adil Rashid, Lawson, from Leeds, had a fluent action. He was deemed surplus to requirements at Yorkshire and tried to prolong his career with other county sides, but nothing worked out. Lawson works as a coach.

Adil Usman Rashid
England, Yorkshire
Born: 17 February 1988, Bradford
First-class: 375 wickets at 34.77

From an early age Rashid looked special. His lively, front-on bowling action was good to watch, as was his batting. He took six wickets on debut for Yorkshire and both his bowling and batting improved over the next couple of years. He joined the England tour of South Africa in 2009/10 but his bowling fell away, with some suggesting it had been tinkered with. His frustrations increased over the next few seasons, leading him at one point to hint he was misunderstood by Yorkshire and wanted to leave. County and player resolved their differences and Rashid's form has returned, allowing him more overs. England picked him again for the 2015 tour of the West Indies.

Max Thomas Charles Waller
Somerset
Born: 3 March 1988, Salisbury, Wiltshire
First-class: 10 wickets at 49.30

Waller has been primarily used in T20 and one-day matches. Opportunities at first-class level have been limited.

William Andrew Thomas Beer
Sussex
Born: 8 October 1988, Crawley, West Sussex
First-class: 13 wickets at 39.92

Another mentee of Terry Jenner, Beer is a gutsy player who gets most opportunities in the shorter forms of the game. He was able to learn from Pakistan's Mushtaq Ahmed in his early days at the club. Beer needs to bowl more in four-day cricket if he is to progress.

Thomas Richard Craddock
Essex
Born: 13 July 1989, Huddersfield, West Yorkshire

Craddock had a good game against England, when they played Essex as a warm-up for the 2013 Ashes, taking five wickets in an innings. But the county laid him off after signing left-arm spinner Monty Panesar from Sussex.

Scott George Borthwick
England, Durham
Born: 19 April 1990, Sunderland
Tests: 4 wickets at 20.50
First-class: 140 wickets at 34.37

One-Test wonder or a star of the future? Borthwick made his debut in the last match of England's appalling Ashes campaign in 2013/14. He gives the ball a rip and plenty of air but lacks overs at seamer-friendly Chester-le-Street, home of his club Durham. Even more than Adil Rashid, he can justify his place at county level as a batsman, usually going in at number three. Now in his mid-20s his role needs to be defined. Is he a batsman who bowls occasionally, or a leg-spinning all-rounder? England need the latter more than the former, especially with the rise of Moeen Ali. Borthwick, an excellent fielder and a chirpy character, needs to bowl, bowl and bowl some more.

All figures correct as of 25 January 2015.

Bibliography

Altham H. and Swanton E., *A History of Cricket*, George, Allen and Unwin Ltd, 1948

Arlott J. (ed), *Cricket: The Great Bowlers*, Pelham Books Ltd, 1968

Atherton M., *Opening Up: My Autobiography*, Hodder & Stoughton, 2002

Bailey T. and Trueman F., *The Spinners' Web*, Collins Willow, 1988

Barry P., *Spun Out: Shane Warne, the Unauthorised Biography of a Cricketing Genius*, Bantam Press, 2006

Beach A., Ferdinands R., Sinclair P., *Measuring Spin Characteristics of a Cricket Ball*, University of Sydney, 2012

Benaud R., *The Appeal of Cricket,* Hodder and Stoughton, 1995

Birley D., *A Social History of English Cricket*, Aurum Press, 1999

Brachfeld O., *Inferiority Feelings: In the Individual and the Group*, Greenwood Press Reprint, 1973

Bradman D., *Farewell to Cricket*, Hodder and Stoughton, 1950

Bradman D., *The Art of Cricket*, Hodder & Stoughton, 1958

Brearley M., *The Art of Captaincy*, Hodder and Stoughton, 1985

Brodribb G., *Next Man In*, Souvenir Press, 1995

Brown F., *Cricket Musketeer*, Nicholas Kaye, 1954

Chalke S. and Hodgson D., *No Coward Soul: The Remarkable Story of Bob Appleyard*, Fairfield Books, 2003

Cowdrey C., *MCC: The Autobiography of a Cricketer*, Hodder and Stoughton, 1976

Dangerfield G., *The Strange Death of Liberal England*, Stanford University Press, 1935

Down M., *Archie: A Biography of AC MacLaren*, George Allen and Unwin, 1981

Duckworth L., *SF Barnes: Master Bowler*, Hutchinson, 1967

Eastaway R., *What is a Googly?*, Robson Books, 1992

Faulkner A., *Cricket: Can It Be Taught?*, Chapman and Hall, 1926

Ferriday P., *Before the Lights Went Out: The 1912 Triangular Tournament*, Von Krumm Publishing, 2011

Fotheringham R., *Exiled to the Colonies: 'Oscar Wilde' in Australia, 1895-1897, Nineteenth Century Theatre and Film, Volume 30, Number 20*, Manchester University Press, 2003

Frith D., *Silence of the Heart: Cricket Suicides*, Mainstream Publishing, 2001

Frith D., *The Slow Men*, Corgi Books, 1985

Fry C. and Beldam G., *Great Bowlers and Fielders: Their Methods at a Glance*, Macmillan, 1906

Goonesena G., *Spin Bowling – The Young Cricketer Talks to G Goonesena*, Phoenix Sports Books, 1959

Grimmett C., *Tricking the Batsman*, Hodder and Stoughton, 1934

Haigh G., *On Warne*, Simon & Schuster, 2012

Hill A., *Daring Young Men*, Methuen, 2005

Hill A., *Jim Laker*, Andre Deutsch, 1998

Hill A., *Johnny Wardle: Cricket Conjuror*, David & Charles, 1988

Hollies E., *I'll Spin You a Tale*, London Museum Press, 1955

Hordern H., *Googlies: Coals from a Test Cricketer's Fireplace*, Angus & Robertson, 1932

Howat G., *Plum Warner*, Unwin Hyman, 1987

Imran Khan, *Imran Khan's Cricket Skills*, Hamlyn, 1989

Jenner T. and Piese K., *TJ Over The Top*, Information Australia, 1999

Karunatilaka S., *Chinaman: The Legend of Pradeep Matthew*, Jonathan Cape, 2011

Knox M., *Bradman's War*, The Robson Press, 2013

Laker J., *Spinning Round the World*, Shakespeare Head Press, 1957

Lemmon D., *Tich Freeman and the Decline of the Leg-Break Bowler*, George Allen & Unwin, 1982

Mailey A., *10 For 66 And All That*, Phoenix House, 1958

Malies J., *Great Characters from Cricket's Golden Age*, Robson Books, 2000

Marriott C., *The Complete Leg-Break Bowler*, Eyre and Spottiswoode, 1968

May P., *A Game Enjoyed*, Stanley Paul, 1985

Meynell L., *Plum Warner*, Phoenix House, 1951

Moult T. (ed), *Bat and Ball: A Book of Cricket*, Magna Books, 1994 (republished from 1935)

Murphy P., *The Spinner's Turn*, J Dent and Sons, 1982

Nichols M., *Bowling,* Blackie and Son Ltd, 1937

Noble M., *Gilligan's Men*, Chapman and Hall, 1925

'An Old Hand', *A Book About Cricket*, Epworth Press, 1924

O'Reilly W., *The Bradman Era*, Willow Books, 1984

O'Reilly W., *'Tiger' O'Reilly: 60 Years in Cricket*, Collins, 1985

Parkin C., *Cricket Triumphs and Troubles*, Nicholls and Co, 1936

Parkinson M., *On Cricket*, Hodder & Stoughton, 2002

Parry R. and Slater D., *The Googly, Gold and the Empire, in Empire and Cricket, The South African Experience 1884 to 1914*, Unisa Press, 2009

Peebles I., *Batter's Castle*, Souvenir Press, 1958

Peebles I., *How to Bowl*, Chapman and Hall, 1934

Peebles I., *Spinner's Yarn*, William Collins Sons and Co, 1977

Peebles I., *The Ashes 1954-5*, Hodder and Stoughton, 1955

Philpott P., *A Spinner's Yarn*, ABC, 1990

Philpott P., *The Art of Wrist-Spin Bowling*, Crowood Press, 2002

Pollard J., *The World's Greatest Leg-Spin Bowlers*, Robert Hale, 1995

Rajan A., *Twirlymen*, Yellow Jersey Press, 2011

Ranjitsinhji K., *Jubilee Book of Cricket*, Thomas Nelson and Sons, 1897

Rayvern Allen D. (ed), *The Essential John Arlott: Forty Years of Classic Cricket Writing*, Guild Publishing, 1989

Sandford C., *Godfrey Evans: A Biography*, Simon and Schuster, 1990

Searle A., *SF Barnes: His Life and Times*, Empire Publications, 1997

Shawcroft J., *History of Derbyshire County Cricket Club*, Christopher Helm, 1989

Steel A. and Lyttleton R., *The Badminton Library of Sports and Pastimes: Cricket*, Longmans, Green and Co, 1888

Swanton E., *Sort of a Cricket Person*, Fontana, 1974

Wallace, J., *100 Greats: Sussex County Cricket Club*, Tempus, 2002

Warne S., *Shane Warne: My Autobiography*, Hodder and Stoughton, 2001

Warner P., *Cricket Across the Seas*, Longmans, Green & Co, 1903

Warner P., *Cricket Between Two Wars*, Sporting Handbooks, 1942

Warner P., *How We Recovered the Ashes, centenary reprint*, Methuen, 2004

Whitington R., *Time of the Tiger: The Bill O'Reilly Story*, Stanley Paul, 1970

Wilkins B., *Cricket: The Bowler's Art*, Kangaroo Press, 1997

Williams C., *Gentlemen & Players: The Death of Amateurism in Cricket*, Phoenix, 2013

Wisden Cricketers' Almanack – various editions

Newspapers and periodicals:

All Out Cricket, Brighton Evening Argus, The Captain, The Cricketer, Daily Express, Daily Mail, Daily Telegraph, The Guardian, Hobart Mercury, Hull Daily Mail, The Independent, The Listener, Nottingham Evening Post, Nightwatchman, The Observer, Sydney Morning Herald, The Times, West Australian Sunday Times, Western Australian, Yorkshire Post

Websites:

BBC Sport, Cricket Archive, ECB, ESPN Cricinfo, MCC, Trove

Index

Massie, Bob 127
May, Peter 104, 106-7, 109-10
MCC 9, 18, 30, 33, 38, 39, 52,
 67, 71, 76, 91, 104,
McCool, Colin 100
McKenzie, Graham 186
Mead, Walter 26, 41, 197-8
Melbourne Cricket Club 38
Mendis, Ajantha 191
Meynell, Lawrence 86
Miller, Keith 95, 116, 154
Mitchell, Tommy 14, 66, 86-7,
 89, 202-3
Moeen Ali 187, 212
Moores, Peter 143
Morris, Arthur 94
Morris, Hugh 159
Mozart, Wolfgang 138
Munday, Michael 8, 163, 165-
 70, 171, 179, 195, 210
Muralitharan, Muttiah 141,
 147, 191
Mushtaq Ahmed 157, 158,
 165-6, 211

Newton, Isaac 48
Nichols, Stan 181
Noble, Monty 48-9, 55-6, 63,
 66

O'Keeffe, Kerry 123
O'Reilly, Bill 13, 23, 37, 55, 64,
 65, 84, 85, 87, 90, 92, 93, 95,
 104, 107, 126, 134, 145, 177
Owen-Smith, 'Tuppy' 81

Panesar, Monty 187-8, 211
Parkin, Cecil 44, 59, 88

Parks, Jim 129
Parliament Act of 1911 24
Parry, Richard 34
Parsons, David 171, 172
Parsons, Jack 102
Peebles, Alastair 9, 78,
Peebles, Ian 10, 14, 39, 51, 55,
 68-76, 77-8, 79, 80-1, 82, 83,
 84, 85, 105, 113, 169, 177,
 182, 203, 205
Peel, Bobby 105
Phillips, Jim 26,
Philpott, Peter 9, 15, 151, 157,
 158, 159, 183, 195-6
Pietersen, Kevin 11, 130, 173-
 4, 188
Pocock, Pat 117
Ponting, Ricky 185
Prior, Matt 188
Procul Harem 116

Queensberry, Marquess of 32

Rajan, Amol 18, 194
Ramadhin, Sonny 119
Ranjitsinhji, KS 21, 33, 35,
 39, 43
Rashid, Adil 171, 171, 188-90,
 210, 211, 212
Reddick, Tommy 82
Rhodes, Wilfred 31, 40, 45,
 55, 58, 104, 105, 200
Rice, Clive 125
Richards, Viv 15, 132
Richmond, Thomas 'Tich' 14,
 66, 200
Rickwood, Gypsy 70
Ring, Doug 95-6